# John of Gaunt

*His Life and Character – Biography of the English Prince, Soldier, Statesman and Political Mediator of the 14th Century*

By C. W. Empson

Published by Pantianos Classics

ISBN-13: 978-1-78987-143-2

First published in 1874

# Contents

*Introduction* .................................................................................. iv
Chapter One - Life of John of Gaunt ........................................ 12
Chapter Two - Character and Influence of John of Gaunt .......... 43
Chief Authorities ........................................................................ 52
**Appendix** .................................................................................. **53**

# Introduction

The fourteenth century, pregnant as it was with organic changes in religion, politics, and industry, forms an important era in English history. The preceding century had witnessed the power of the Church at its height, the following its downfall, while throughout this the change was slowly taking place. Simultaneously the people struggled successfully after liberty, and emerged from a state of darkness into that light, which had so long been denied them by their priestly rulers. The spirit of enterprise, which had remained dormant for ages, now sprung up with renewed vigour, and the impoverished coffers of the kingdom began to be refilled. These were no slight or unimportant revolutions, but made themselves felt in all the relations of life. As the improvements resulted from the power of the Church being gradually confined within proper limits, it will be well to briefly survey the leading points of the current religious history.

When the sceptre of England was in the feeble hands of John and Henry III., the Papal extortions knew no bounds; livings and canonries were disposed of to foreigners and strangers, who never betrayed any interest in their benefices, far less visited them. The sole object of the Pope seemed to be to gather money into the hands of the Church, and, too often, into his own. But with the accession of Edward I., indisputably the greatest of the Plantagenets, the order of things changed. He saw the clergy usurping every office, he saw the wealth of the realm pouring away into foreign countries, and determined to put a stop to all this in the interest of the nation. With consummate skill he shifted the odium of persecution from his own shoulders to those of his subjects. He placed the clergy out of the pale of the law, enjoining his judges to give every man justice against them, but them justice against none. Those who will not contribute to the support of my government must not expect to reap the benefit of its protection; so ran the rigorous logic of this resolute politician. The distress of the clergy was great; any man who had a grudge against them might indulge his anger with impunity, and do endless damage to the property of his enemy. Edward, moreover, caused the famous Statute of Mortmain to be passed forbidding at the same time the exportation of the proceeds of any English benefice or abbey. These wise laws were confirmed by Edward III., who added many minor ones to give more detail to the general regulations of his predecessors, while in 1392 the Statute of Praemurine became part of our Constitution. In 1371 the Parliament petitioned the King to fill the highest offices of State with laymen instead of ecclesiastics, [A] and William of Wykeham, who was then Chancellor, resigned his post. There was much reason for the popular outcry against the Church, apart from the great covetousness it displayed. The power and riches of the English clergy, had, it is true, been increasing beyond all precedent: the owners of half the landed estate in England, they also possessed personal property of untold value. Had this wealth been wisely and liberally employed for the benefit of the people, all might have remained unchanged for ages longer. The bishops held high offices of State to the prejudice of their sees, where the secular clergy were living in a deplorable condition of laxness and immorality, which completely lost them the respect of the people. The monasteries, too, had fallen grievously from the standard of purity and simplicity proposed by their founders, They because the resort of men who wished to have their private pleasures curtailed as little as possible, while they enjoyed the peace and security afforded by these sanctuaries. So gross and notorious was the conduct of both seculars and regulars, [B] that the Pope felt bound to save the honour and dignity of his name by attempting to stem the torrent of vice. For this purpose he commissioned the Mendicant Friars, who numbered many energetic and restless men in their ranks, to cross over to England. Bound by a vow of poverty, and clothed in the humblest of dress, they presented the greatest conceivable contrast to the wealthy ecclesiastics. Addressing the people in plain homely language, they speedily gained an influence over them, such as the seculars, with their laboured, monotonous discourses, unintelligible to the common people, had never attained. But in time they also fell into evil courses, corrupted by the luxury that met them on every hand, and, quarrelling among themselves, united only to abuse the regulars. When the teachers of religion were thus sunk in wickedness, when two rival Popes disputed the ecclesiastical supremacy, when indulgences were granted to the greatest criminals, if only they paid high enough for them, no wonder people sighed for a purer faith, and welcomed the advent of Wickliffe Langland and Chaucer launched biting sarcasms against the iniquity of the clergy; nor does the latter's picture of the Pardonere at all exaggerate the extent of the evil. [C]

The profoundly superstitious age was now past, when men were unable to resist the effects of an excommunication, so that they no longer feared to maintain the rights of their country against the encroachments of the Church. It is only fair to add, that the prelates of England, however covetous and avaricious they might be when their own interests were concerned, often showed themselves no less ready to uphold the rightful authority of the Crown, than to defend their own ancient privileges in the face of Papal interference. The latter half of the fourteenth century was the time of continual struggle between the clergy and the Lollards, as the followers of Wickliffe were called. Whatever opinions we may hold with reference to Wickliffe's doctrines, we cannot but acknowledge the singular adaptation of means to his end. The Romish Church delighted in gorgeous ritual; Wickliffe advocated the simplest and plainest service possible. Its clergy were possessed of enormous wealth; he taught that the ministers of religion should imitate the primitive poverty of the Apostles. It regarded the Pope as the representative of Christ on earth; he denounced him as Anti-Christ. It issued pardons, indulgences, excommunications, absolutions; he declared these were the invention of the devil. Lastly, its great doctrine was that of Transubstantiation; he entirely rejected it. In short, in every way possible, he presented the greatest contrast to the Romish Church. Ignorant men might be unable to distinguish between the rival doctrines, but no one could mistake the difference between the simple service of one party, and the ornate service of the other. Still he was only incomplete. He destroyed the existing system, but did not reconstruct a new one. Yet the minds of the people were ripe for a change, and nearly half the population were accounted. Lollards. It was the vicious lives that the clergy were leading that precipitated this revolution of feeling, and caused men to rebel against the authority of the Church sooner than they would otherwise have done.

Nor was this laxity of morals and general licentiousness confined to the clergy; unhappily it pervaded all ranks of society. This so-called age of chivalry was disgraced by the most bare-faced vice, an accomplished knight enjoying the same prerogatives as were claimed by the dissolute courtiers of Charles 11. or Louis XV. [1] In the dawn of chivalry a sort of material love for our Lady was fostered in the minds of warriors; she was the guide of their actions, the pole star of their affections. From this the transition to a high regard for, and a deference to ladies was easy. But as time went on, love almost entirely took the place of respect, and when that barrier was broken down, the fiery spirits of the knights knew no restraint. Open licentiousness became the rule, instead of the exception, as the old poets and romancers only too plainly show.

But in spite of this, the feelings of loyalty, courtesy, and liberality were not extinct; nor are we at a loss to point out men of this century, who were pre-eminent as mirrors of chivalry. Foremost of their day stand Edward III., the Black Prince, and Bertrand du Guesclin, while round them were gathered a brilliant crowd, scarcely inferior in reputation: Henry, Duke of Lancaster, the Captal de Buche, Lord Chandos, Sir John Hawkwood, Sir Walter Manny, are names that will readily occur to all. Such noble and heroic characters as these shine with such brilliancy, that we are apt at first to believe that they, were the more prominent in an age when each man was a hero. But when we examine facts with care, we find that in every period heroic persons were few in number, while the rest were too often covetous and perjured. The zenith of chivalry seems ever in the past, [D] yet if the code of knighthood had at any time real influence in England, surely it was in the reign of Edward III. But enough of knights and their prowess; let us turn for a brief space to the humbler affairs of the people.

During this century a great impulse was given to the cause of liberty, after which we find the lower orders of Europe constantly struggling. The Italian republics had in most cases attained a fair degree of freedom, but were beginning to lose it, and at this time it is very hard to distinguish between their popular risings and party quarrels. Still in 1378, when Salvestro de Medici was Gonfalonier of

Justice at Florence, there was an undoubted insurrection, caused by the imposition of an obnoxious law. It was quelled for a time, but a month afterwards the Ciompi, or lowest populace, broke out in rebellion again, and placed one of their order, Michel di Lando, in power. Fortunately, although of humble birth, he was a moderate and able man, and managed to restore order, acting in all things so fairly, that he was accused of betraying the popular cause. The result of these disturbances was that the Guelf chiefs learned so much wisdom, that by ruling in tolerable accordance with the laws, they were able to maintain their power for half a century. [2]

In Rome the impassioned eloquence of Rienzi obtained such a mastery over the people, that they rose in 1347, and expelled the nobles, appointing Rienzi their tribune. This lasted but for a time, and then Rienzi was compelled to give up his rule, being thrown into prison at Avignon. Becoming possessed again of the supreme power by a strange freak of fortune, he behaved so tyrannically that he was murdered in 1364. [3]

In France a terrible insurrection broke out in 1358, owing to the misery of the peasants, aggravated as it was by the insolence and luxury of their lords. This rising was called the Jacquerie, from the phrase "Jacques bon homme," applied to men of the lower orders. In their unbridled rage they committed indescribable atrocities, and were not suppressed without the greatest difficulty. A most lamentable picture of the state of France in 1360, is drawn by Petrarch, who visited Paris during that year. He says that the neighbourhood of Paris manifested everywhere marks of destruction and conflagration; that the streets were deserted, and the whole a vast solitude. [4]

In 1381 the Flemings rebelled, owing to the town of Ghent being taxed without its consent by Louis, Count of Flanders. Under the leadership of the celebrated Philip Yan Artevelde, the burghers took the field, distinguishing themselves by their bravery and address. [E] It was not till the Count of Flanders had obtained the powerful aid of the King of France that he was able to subdue them. While Charles VI. was absent on this expedition, an insurrection broke out among the Parisians, which he put down with the greatest severity on his return. There can be but little doubt, that, had he been defeated by the Flemings, this rising would have spread over the whole of France, [5] In the same year the famous riot of Wat

Tyler broke out in England; his followers were of the lowest class, as is shown by the humorous description of Gower. [F]

In the early part of this century the Swiss boldly resisted the encroachments of the Austrian Emperor, and, after some minor engagements, completely defeated him at Morgarten. This victory procured the three allied cantons of Uri, Schweitz, and Unterwalden their liberty, which they have maintained up to the present day. Such is a brief notice of the chief popular risings of the age.

One of the most striking features of this century was a passion for luxury which was carried to a ruinous excess. [6] One of the Parliaments of Edward IIL passed no less than eight laws against French fashions. The Black Death had so largely depopulated the country that the prosperity of the working classes had risen enormously, and the attempts of the legislation to fix a maximum of wages were fruitless. It had the good effect of giving an immense impulse to, if it did not actually create, the spirit of enterprise. Commercial companies began to be established, while the consular system advanced rapidly in importance. [G] The Hanseatic league obtained command of the Baltic, and, by the treaty of Stralsund, in 1370, made commercial interests dominant in the North; while the Venetians in the South proved no unworthy followers in its footsteps. Ships were enabled to navigate the seas more freely by the aid of the compass, which now came into general use; while the invention of gunpowder completely altered all military tactics, for it removed the vast superiority that knights formerly had over common soldiers.

Invention and commercial activity were the order of the day, as the passion for luxury was not easily satisfied. This industrial spirit had much to do with the downfall of the Church in England, as well as elsewhere. The wise policy ci Edward III. drew weavers, dyers, and fullers from Flanders and other parts of Europe on promises of protection and encouragement. Many of these immigrants were refugees holding the faith of the Albigenses, for which they had suffered grievous persecutions at the hands of the Pope, and it is largely owing to their earnest desire for a translation of the Bible, that Wickliffe's version was produced. The great battle, however, between industry and the Church was fought on the question of usury, which was pronounced absolutely wrong by the clergy. The Church lost the day and her defeat weakened her hold on the people to a large extent, as her doctrine on usury had been very obstinately adhered to, and considered fundamental

There is but one more thing to which I would allude, and that is the language and literature of England during this period. At its beginning we had no national language, but used a sort of fusion of Anglo-Saxon and Anglo-Norman, which in time became a distinct language, and that the language of England. The Norman-French that had been the court language fell into disuse with great rapidity during the French wars of Edward III, owing to the intense hatred engendered by them in the English against anything French,

Robert Langland, John Gower, Geoffrey Chaucer, were the most prominent of the poets who inaugurated a new school of poetry and a more elegant form of language. Instead of the subject being taken from the lives of saints and martyrs, it was inspired by the occurrences of every-day life or the beauties of nature.

Chaucer was no secluded hermit, but a thorough man of the world, a traveller, and a frequenter of the court. His poems ring with the true notes of experience, gathered in the stirring scenes of life, and are consequently full of interest and liveliness, where his monkish predecessors prosed away in inharmonious dulness. The freshness, vigour, and melody of his versification are far in excess of any of the poets who wrote before him, or, indeed, of his own time. Langland, however, excelled him in political satires, as a perusal of "Piers the Ploughman" with its keen irony and biting sarcasms will soon convince the reader.

I have now sketched briefly some of the leading movements of the age, so that the position of actors in it may be made clearer.

The statesman whose life I have to examine — John of Gaunt — is one who is usually more or less passed over, and it will be seen that I think this omission is partly justifiable, though not wholly so. I am only aware of two writers who have given at all a full account of his life — Collins and Godwin. The former gives the principal events of his life in dry detail, hardly attempting to connect them, but jotting down each as they occur. Godwin's account is much fuller, but is mixed up very largely with discussions on Chaucer and his poems, so that the life of John of Gaunt has to be evolved out of disconnected chapters and paragraphs. I have, accordingly, thought it best to compile a life of John of Gaunt from the best sources at my disposal, leaving his character and influence to be examined in another chapter.

[1] St. Falaye, Mém. sur la Chevalerie ii., 69.
[2] Hallam's Hist. Middle Ages, i., 439.
[3] Milman, Hist. Lat. Christ, v. 517.
[4] Mém. de Petrarque, t. iii., p. 541.
[5] Froissart, vol. i., c. 120.
[6] Lecky's History of Rationalism, i., 311.

# Chapter One - Life of John of Gaunt

John of Gaunt, the fourth son of Edward III. and Philippa of Hainault, was born at Ghent towards the end of February, 1340. [H] He. was created Earl of Richmond, September 20th, 1342, having therewith a grant in tail general of all the castles, manors, and lands belonging to that earldom, and all the prerogatives and royalties which John, late Duke of Brittany and Richmond, had enjoyed. [1] The next mention we find of him is in 1345, when a charter was granted to him for a market every week at his manor at Bassingbourne, and also at Badburham, the former place being allowed in addition to have a fair once a year for seven days on the eve of Saint Peter and Saint Paul.

Of his early life nothing is definitely known, and we naturally assume it was spent after the manner of the age. It was the custom then for all scions of noble houses to be brought up with a view to adopting either the military or the clerical profession. If, as in the present case, the former was selected, the boy became a page at the age of seven, and was sent to the castle of some baron famous for his bravery and wisdom. In the case of wealthy parents, he would usually remain at home, poorer children being received as companions for him in his education. He was to learn modesty, obedience, courtesy to ladies, and address in arms and horsemanship. He was taught to regard knighthood as the great aim of his life, and to reverence it aa a sacred institution, sanctified by the rites and ordinances of the Church. He had to attend his lord in the chase, and in short, to use the language of the day, "the gentle damosel learned to bear the fatigue, hunger, and thirst of a practised woodsman." He bore a chivalrous regard to the ladies and their fair name, attaching himself more especially to one as his mistress, to whom he was bound to render any service in his power. This period of probation lasted until he was fourteen, when he was considered qualified to discharge the duties of a squire. He then became the personal attendant of his lord in battle, accoutering him for the fight, and leading a spare horse as a remount, should the war horse become disabled. It was his office to see that all the armour of the knight he followed was in good order, so as to stand the numerous shocks it was subjected to. At the age of twenty-one the order of knighthood might be conferred upon him, and the ceremony was invested with all the pomp and solemnity the religious services of the Church could give. The ties between a knight and his squires were so very close and intimate that they often lasted by courtesy long after they had by right been dissolved.

There is good reason for supposing that John of Gaunt was page and squire to his uncle Henry, Earl of Lancaster; not only was that leader of the highest military reputation, but he was also of royal blood. It would seem, therefore, highly probable that the training of the King's sons would be entrusted to him, and indeed we find them continually accompanying him on his foreign expeditions. John of Gaunt may, too, have singled out his cousin Blanche, Henry's daughter and his future wife, as his mistress during this early part of his life. All this, however, is but conjecture, without legitimate proof and must be taken as such. The period of probation for a squire, it has been said, was usually from fourteen to twenty-one. Nevertheless, in the case of the royal blood and other distinguished personages, the time of probation was not infrequently shortened, and we find John of Gaunt knighted on the downs of Kent, in November, 1355, when he was just under sixteen years of age. He was knighted, together with his brother Lionel and twenty-five other squires, before Edward started on an expedition to France, whither both John of Gaunt and Lionel proceeded with Henry, Duke of Lancaster. This attack on the northern provinces of France was made to distract the attention of the French from the proceedings of the Black Prince, who was ravaging the country between Bordeaux and the Pyrenees. But King John of France, though at the head of a large army, refused to accept the battle which Edward continually offered him, and finally compelled his opponent to retreat to Calais to obtain provisions. He contrived to keep him there for several days, amusing him with the notion of a general battle to come off at some indefinite time Edward, however, suddenly returned to England [I] on hearing that the Scots had seized the opportunity given them by his absence to invade England and revenge their defeat at Neville's Cross. He was accompanied by his sons, John of Gaunt and Lionel, and, after being present at Parliament, on November 25th, proceeded straight to Berwick, which he reached about the middle of January, 1356. [2] The south of Scotland became the theatre of his operations, and incalculable damage was done by his troops to the country round Edinburgh — so much so that the people spoke of Candlemass that year as "The Burned Candlemass." Edward had previously purchased all Baliol's rights [J] to the throne of Scotland for 5,000 marks, and an annuity of £2,000; the deed of transfer was dated from Roxburgh, [3] and had appended to it the names of John of Gaunt and Lionel, signing themselves Earls of Richmond and Ulster, respectively, as witnesses. He returned to England with his sons during the spring of 1356.

The movements of John of Gaunt are now shrouded in obscurity till December 1357, when we have indirect evidence that he was on a visit to his faster-in-law, the wife of Lionel, at Hatfield, in Yorkshire, for we know she presented new year's gifts to his cook and clerk of the kitchen. [K] It was here in all probability that the great event of his life — his marriage with Blanche, co-heiress of Henry, Duke of Lancaster — was first thought of. There is little doubt but that she was living at Axholme, the seat of Lord Mowbray, her uncle by marriage, Lady Mowbray being Lady Ulster's aunt on the mother's side; for we find Lady Ulster, this autumn, giving money to a servant of the Duke of Lancaster, for bringing over a letter from Blanche. [L] Chaucer informs us that John of Gaunt's proposal of marriage was rejected by her at first, but was accepted after another year had elapsed. As his marriage took place May 19th, 1359, the date of his first proposal to her might very well be some time in the early spring of 1358. It was here, too, that the first traces of his connection with Chaucer are discoverable; for the poet was a page in Lionel's household. After the lapse of a year, during which time [M] we may assume John of Gaunt was more or less in attendance on Blanche, she was induced to A.D. listen to his entreaties, and his marriage was solemnized 1359. at Reading, on May 19th, 1359, with great state, a dispensation having been previously obtained from the Pope. [4] The following week a grand tournament was held at London in their honour, the mayor, sheriffs, and court of aldermen challenging all comers. The challengers were represented by the King, his four sons and nineteen great barons of England, a condescension on the part of the royal family that highly gratified the citizens.

A treaty had been signed March 24th, between Edward and John, King of France, who was then a prisoner in England, but the States had refused to ratify it. The result of this refusal was that Edward resumed active hostilities, and sailed from Sandwich, in Kent, October 28th, with a great armament computed at 1,000 ships and 100,000 men. He was accompanied by his four eldest sons, Chaucer, the poet, being attached to the train of Lionel. No less than seven weeks were spent in a fruitless siege of Rheims before an advance was made on Paris. Neither the Duke of Lancaster nor John of Gaunt were, however, idle, for they were detached on a special expedition to harass the enemy and ravage the country, a commission which they executed with great success. The English army reached Paris March 31st, and encamped there for thirteen days, but, not being strong enough to besiege the town, and being unable to persuade the Dauphin to come out to battle, was compelled to retreat to Brittany. Their retreat was conducted amid much suffering owing to fatigue and want of provisions, their misfortunes culminating in a terrific storm of thunder and lightning which broke over them near Calais, and for a while unnerved even the iron Edward. These troubles induced him to consent to peace, and the necessary papers were signed [5] at Bretigni near Chartres, May 8th. Edward and his sons, however, remained in France till October 24th, when John, King of France came over from England and ratified the treaty with solemn oaths, soon after which Edward returned to England. The articles were signed with great religious ceremonies, the Archbishop of Canterbury conducting a special service at which the King and his sons were present. [6]

During the year 1360, John of Gaunt [N] was made one of the Knight Companions of the Garter, in the room of Thomas Holland, Earl of Kent, one of the original founders, who had died December 28th, 1359. The exact time of his appointment is uncertain, but it probably was after April 23rd, for robes of the order were directed to be provided for him, under the title of Earl of Richmond, for the *first* time, against the Feast of St. George (April 23rd), 1361.

He had hardly come of age when Henry, Duke of Lancaster, died of the plague, March 24th, leaving his vast possessions to be divided between his two daughters, Blanche and Maud. The King issued a charter [O] bearing date November 13th, 1361, to John of Gaunt, granting divers privileges to himself and his heirs by Blanche, in the lands of the duchy which he had inherited. By a strange vitality, Maud, who had married the Duke of Bavaria died childless in the following year, and consequently her interest in the Duchy of Lancaster devolved upon Blanche, whose husband, John of Gaunt, became the wealthiest landowner in England.[P] Indeed, so much did he gain by her death, that the historian Knighton [Q] charges him with having poisoned Maud, "for the sake of restoring to the inheritance of her father its full integrity," but there is no evidence to support this view, which must be regarded as a speculation, and not as a proved fact.

On May 12th, 1362, he procured a charter from the King, granting to him the same rights in Maud's property as he had by the charter of November 13th, 1361, in Blanche's; and the King farther favoured him by creating him Duke of Lancaster, [R] so that his style now was, Duke of Lancaster, Earl of Richmond, Leicester, Lincoln, and Derby. [7] His brother Lionel was at the same time created Duke of Clarence, and despatched to Ireland on service. In connection with this expedition we find the Government issuing strict orders to John of Gaunt to prohibit the export of provisions of various kinds from Liverpool, as well as dyewares, "worstedes," sea coal, and afterwards horses, linen, jewels, and precious metals.

On July 14th, 1364, the King granted to John of Gaunt a charter, [S] renewing the old charter granted to Henry, Earl of Lancaster, May 7th, 1342, whereby large liberties were acquired; but it was specially enacted that this charter should apply only to those lands which belonged to the Earl of Lancaster on May 14th, 1342.

The Black Prince had left England, January, 1363, for Aquitaine, [8] which had been given to him as a fief the previous year, and Lionel was absent in Ireland, so that John of Gaunt and Edmund of Langley were the only grown-up sons of Edward remaining in England during the years 1363-4-5. The former had, therefore, a magnificent opportunity for ingratiating himself with his father, and he did not lose it. His brother Edmund, being only "a soft prince," [9] in no way interfered with him, but allowed him to acquire power without opposition. The way was already paved for him, as he had all along been the favourite son of Edward, and now that the counteracting influence of the Black Prince was removed, he rapidly rose to the post of chief adviser to his father.

During 1364 he and Edmund visited Lewis, Earl of Flanders, in hopes of arranging a treaty of marriage between Edmund and the Duchess of Burgundy, the Earl's daughter; the articles and contract were executed October 19th, but the match was in the end broken off.

The year 1366 was marked by an event which subsequently influenced the whole course of John of Gaunt's life — namely, the deposition of Pedro the Cruel, King of Castile, and his appeal for help to the Black Prince. To understand this fully we must go back a year or two. The Black Prince had left England for Aquitaine, in February, 1363, where he had been ever since, holding his court at Bordeaux.

In this age of chivalry, so chivalrous a character attracted great admiration, and his court was thronged with knights of all nations, anxious to share some of his renown. Nor did kings consider it beneath them to visit him as though he were their equal Peter of Cyprus, James of Majorca, Charles of Navarre, passed several weeks with him in Aquitaine. Everything that was noble or chivalrous was collected round him, so that his became the most brilliant court in Christendom. While he was ruling his province with a firm hand, the kingdom of France was suffering immensely from the ravages of the Great Company. During the wars between England and France, each King had employed large numbers of mercenaries, Edward having the most, simply because he was the richer. On the conclusion of peace, these troops were paid off, and their occupation was gone. They were accustomed to a free roving life, and no other had any charms for them, so they determined to make war on their own account, and enact the part of modem Ishmaelites. This they did with considerable success, defeating an army, commanded by John de Bourbon, sent against them by Charles V., King of France, and ravaging his dominions. If Charles trembled at Paris, not less so did the Pope at Avignon; indeed, on one occasion, a troop of these banditti, led by the famous Araldo di Cervola, forced the latter to redeem himself by a payment of 4,000 crowns. Edward III. engaged to clear the country of them, but Charles V. had no wish to see another English army in his territories, and eventually declined the offer, after he had once accepted it. Charles at last devised a plan of getting rid of them. Pedro the Cruel, King of Castile, had, by his cruelties, provoked an insurrection of his subjects, which, however, he was able to quell the leaders (amongst whom were his two illegitimate half-brothers, Enrique of Transtamare, and Tello, Count of Biscay,) fled to Arragon. Pedro pursued them thither, and compelled them to seek an asylum in France, where they were hospitably received by Charles V, who intended making use of them to carry off the Great Company. It was carefully represented to them that with these veterans they could easily overcome Pedro, and get possession of his dominions, and they took the advice. [T] It was, however, first necessary to obtain an able leader, in whom the Free Companies had confidence, and the man for the purpose evidently was Bertrand Duguesclin, who was at the time a prisoner in England. The Pope, Charles V. of France, and Enrique of Transtamare, joined together to pay the ransom demanded for him — 100,000 francs. [10] Besides this, considerable sums were given to the Free Companies, the Pope being an unwilling contributor to the amount of 200,000 livres; he had wanted them to remain satisfied with his blessing, but he was assured that the Companies could make shift without absolution, but not without money. [11] They at last marched off to Spain, and Pedro was obliged to fly without fighting a Rattle. He fled to Bordeaux with his daughters, where he implored help from the Black Prince to enable him to regain his throne. His prayers were favourably listened to, and the Black Prince sent messengers to Edward III. [U] to learn what he advised. On October 24th, 1366, John of Gaunt left England for Bordeaux with reinforcements consisting of, according to Froissart, [12] 400 men-at-arms and 400 archers. He was instructed to consent in Edward's name to assistance being rendered to Pedro. [V] What induced Edward to assist Pedro is uncertain, it may have been the recollection that the latter would have been his son-in-law, had not his daughter died at Bayonne on her way to Spain, it may have been a chivalrous feeling for an exiled king, and a cordial dislike of an usurper. No conjecture, however, seems more likely than the simple one that hatred of the French was the real motive. Pedro had married Blanche, sister-in-law of the King of France, and had treated her so shamefully that Charles had vowed revenge. [W] He was fortunate enough to be able to gratify his vengeance, and to rid his dominions at the same time of the Great Company. The French indirectly, if not directly, [X] ranged themselves on the side of Enrique, what more natural than that the English should be found on that of Pedro?

The necessary preparations for the expedition were soon made, and the English left Bordeaux January 5th, 1367, *en route* for Spain. The Black Prince had previously recalled all Frenchmen, serving under Duguesclin, whom he was entitled to influence, and so many obeyed his summons, out of their great admiration of his character, that Duguesclin was compelled to winter in France. The English armies entered the passes of the Pyrenees towards the end of February, and steadily continued their march to Castile, forming, on the way, a compulsory alliance with the King of Navarre, which proved most useful to them. John of Gaunt, with Lord Chandos as coadjutor, commanded that part of the Great Company which was in Edward's pay. [Y] The forces of Pedro and Enrique met at Najara, [13] and a bloody battle ensued, which resulted in the latter's complete discomfiture. The mercenaries of John of Gaunt were opposed to those of Duguesclin, and bore the brunt of the engagement, composing as they did the vanguard of the English army. [Z] [A1] The Castillians willingly returned to their allegiance, and Pedro was duly reseated on his throne. [B2] And now the treachery and bad faith of that King became only too apparent; he pleaded poverty as an excuse for non-payment of the sums of money he had promised, and induced the Black Prince to encamp at Valladolid — a notoriously unhealthy place — by promising him he would collect the money as soon as possible. What he wished happened. While he was carefully abstaining from fulfilling his promise, the Black Prince and his army, after suffering from all kinds of disease during June, July, and August of this year, were finally compelled to retreat to Bordeaux. The Black Prince having made himself responsible for the money Pedro had promised to pay, was consequently heavily in debt on Pedro failing to keep his word. In order to meet his liabilities, he levied a tax on hearths in Aquitaine, which created the more discontent as taxation was at this early period quite a novelty in government. Many complaints were made to the King of France, who seized this favourable opportunity to check the growing power of the English, and, in direct defiance of the treaty of Bretigny, summoned the Black Prince to appear before him at Paris. As the A.D. Black Prince indignantly refused to comply, a new war naturally broke out between England and France. [14] In the beginning of September, 1369, [15] John of Gaunt crossed over from Dover to Calais with a large force, [C2] accompanied by Sir Walter Manny, but he effected nothing, for the French pursued a Fabian policy, and he returned to England in November. During this year he experienced a severe loss in the death of his wife Blanche, who died, like her father, of the plague. His marriage with her had been one of pure affection, and he seems to have cherished her with the most devoted love. No one who has read Chaucer's "Dream" can fail to have been struck with the affecting tenderness with which the mourning knight tells the tale of his love and his loss; how utterly he refuses to be comforted, and with what melancholy pleasure he dwells on the happiness he once had, but which has suddenly been taken away. Nor may we doubt the truth of Chaucer's account; it was written during the life-time of John of Gaunt, with whom he was on terms of the most intimate friendship; [D2] nothing could have been more distasteful to his patron than to have such feelings attributed to him when he never felt them. Charles V. had meanwhile confiscated the English possessions in France, and the inhabitants of Aquitaine, being ill-affected towards England, in no way resented this action. He artfully fomented their discontent, and at length despatched two armies, which succeeded, among other things, in capturing the town of Limoges, through the treachery of its bishop. The Dukes of Anjou and Berri marched on the Black Prince from opposite points. This fairly roused him, and, ill as he was, he took the field. John of Gaunt had arrived, with his brother Edmund, [E2] early in the summer, and the three' brothers attacked Limoges, vowing vengeance on its inhabitants. The town speedily succumbed, and a general massacre took place, no mercy being shown, except to a small band of gallant knights, who with their backs to a wall, determined to sell their lives as dearly as possible. John of Gaunt, Edmund, and the Earl of Pembroke singled out the commander and two of his friends as their opponents, and so obstinately did they continue the struggle, that the Black Prince was filled with admiration, and relenting, gave them that quarter which the entreaties of women and children had failed to obtain. The arch traitor, the bishop, was reserved for the special vengeance of the Prince, which would have been executed but for the interference of John of Gaunt, who managed to obtain the guardianship of the prelate's person. He then wrote to the Pope, asking him to beg the bishop's pardon from the Black Prince, which was most unwillingly granted.

As a reward for his various services, John of Gaunt received from the Black Prince a grant of the castle, town, and chastellanie of La Roche-sur-Yon, October 8th, 1370. Great exertions had been made in England to equip John of Gaunt for this expedition to France. Adam de Hoghton, Roger de Pilkington, William de Atherton, Richard de Radclyf, and Matthew de Rixton, commissioners of array for the county of Lancaster, were appointed by Royal Mandate in 1370 [16] to press and enrol 400 archers in Lancashire to accompany John of Gaunt to Aquitaine, and all were informed that John had been appointed Sling's Captain and Lieutenant in "Guynes and Caleys." A month after, the sheriff was ordered to array ail capable fighting men, between sixteen and sixty, to resist the French who threatened to invade England, to obstruct the passage of merchants and merchandise, and to "abolish the English language!" Orders were also issued to seize ail vessels of from twelve to forty tons burthen between Liverpool and Chester inclusive, for the purpose of transporting this levy of men to Southampton and Plymouth, whence the expedition was to sail on May 26th, 1370.

Early in 1371 the failing health of the Black Prince compelled him to sail with his princess to England, leaving John of Gaunt to act as his deputy in Aquitaine, and to perform the obsequies of his eldest son, who had just died, aged only seven. John of Gaunt had hardly assumed the reins of government before the powerful lord of Montpaon revolted, and tried to incite the French party to support him. But the Prince with great promptitude marched on Montpaon, captured the place, and crushed the rebellion, the leader, however, managing to make good his escape.

During his rule in Aquitaine, John of Gaunt married Constance, the elder daughter of Pedro, King of Spain, while Edmund married the younger. [F2] These ladies had for some years been visitors at the court of the Black Prince, and were now fatherless, Pedro having been murdered by Enrique in 1368. It is said that this marriage was entered upon by the advice of Sir Guischard D'Angle, a faithful knight of Aquitaine. However this may be, the importance of the event can hardly be over-rated. John of Gaunt, in right of his wife, styled himself King of Castile and Leon, assuming the insignia. His was, nevertheless, merely a speculative claim, like that of Edward III. to the throne of France, and it proved nearly as disastrous to England, since he continually wished to make expeditions to gain what he held to be his rights. At the end of this year he returned to England with Constance, leaving the Captal de Buche in chaise of Aquitaine. [G2]

This year (1371) was marked by an attack made in Parliament by the laity on the clergy, a petition being presented to the King, asking him to fill the highest offices of State with laymen, instead of ecclesiastics. It has been said that John of Gaunt was at the bottom of this proceeding, [H2] and there appears much truth in the statement. It must not, however, be supposed that he was induced to support the cause of the laity owing to hatred of William of Wykeham; this view has been clearly shown to be erroneous by Lowth. [17] No doubt as politicians they were opposed, Wykeham belonging to what might be called the Conservative, John of Gaunt to the Liberal party, and each would naturally try to curtail the political power of the other. Still, if there had been any dislike or hatred involved, John of Gaunt, on going to France, would never have appointed William of Wykeham, as he did both in 1369 and 1373, to be one of the trustees of the custody, and entire management of all the revenues of his castles, manors, and estates, fix>m one year after his own decease, in order to the payment of his debts, and for other uses as he should direct; while in 1375 he constituted the same bishop his attorney, together with the Earl of Arundel, to appear and act for him in any of the Courts of England during his absence at the Congress of Bruges. Such proofs of confidence never would have been shown to anyone who was in any way regarded as an enemy, and political rivalry does not imply private enmity. The King consented to the petition of his faithful Commons, and William of Wykeham resigned the Great Seals, which he then held, to be succeeded by Sir Robert de Thorp. Wickliffe was actively engaged in this controversy, [I2] He published a pamphlet, [J2] where he speaks of himself as one of the royal chaplains, asserting that the various demands made on England by the Pope were illegal and unconstitutional. This writing of his was issued with authority, for he had been invited by the Crown to give his opinion on the subject.

In the year 1372, John of Gaunt resigned the earldom of Richmond, receiving in exchange other estates from the King, who also caused him to be summoned to Parliament (Oct. 6) by the title of King of Castila The assumption of this title had previously given great umbrage [18] to Enrique of Transtamare, the reigning monarch, who promptly resented the act by allying himself closely with the King of France, and sending a fleet of forty ships to Rochelle, where they engaged the Earl of Pembroke, completely defeating him. This blow sunk the spirits of the English, and proportionately raised those of the French, who overran Aquitaine without meeting much opposition. On September 29th, Edward III., accompanied by the Black Prince and John of Gaunt, sailed from England to relieve the town of Thenars, which was then closely invested by the French forces under Duguesclin. But the weather proved so unpropitious that the expedition had to be given up, and Thouars was compelled to capitulate. In the following year, John of Gaunt crossed to France, determined, if possible, to stem the torrent of these successes. Assembling a large force of 30,000 men he marched from Calais in the early part of November, and traversed France to Bordeaux without being able to provoke a battle. Sir Robert Knolles ably supported him, and insulted the very walls of Paris, but nothing would induce Charles to risk an engagement, though he seized every opportunity of cutting off stragglers and otherwise annoying the English army. [K2] No material good resulted from this march of John of Gaunt; Charles pursued a waiting policy, in the face of which his adversary could do nothing. John of Gaunt returned to England in July, 1374, and had the mortification of hearing that as soon as he had left France all Aquitaine deserted the English King. [L2]

Early in 1375 he went over to Bruges with Sudbury, Bishop of London, and William, Earl of Salisbury, to confer with the French commissioners, the Dukes of Anjou and Burgundy, on the possibility of establishing peace between England and France. He was unsuccessful, however, [M2] though the Pope sent two ecclesiastics as mediators — the Archbishop of Ravenne and the Bishop of Carpentras.

Still there was one thing which John of Gaunt might congratulate himself upon — viz., the adjustment of the English clergy question. A solemn embassy had been despatched in 1373 to the Pope at Avignon to try to settle amicably the great question of the dual allegiance of the clergy, and the Pope had invited the English to send commissioners to meet his own [N2] at Bruges, in the following year. The King then appointed the Bishop of Bangor, Wickliffe, [02] and five others to represent him; the result of their conference with the Papal legatees was the issuing of six bulls [19] by Gregory XI., dated September, 1375, settling the question.

Since the year 1374, John of Gaunt had been all powerful in England, and is fairly entitled to the credit of having satisfactorily brought the affair to a conclusion. He, however, showed his desire to humble the clergy by allowing the Pope to demand from them 100,000 florins [20] in composition for the various subsidies imposed on them on various pretences, and as a reward for his services he presented Wickliffe with the living of Lutterworth.

The position of affairs in England in 1376, was very critical The King was weak and feeble, the Black Prince dying, and all eyes were turned on John of Gaunt, who after those, was the natural guardian of the realm, being the next of blood to the throne who was of full age. His party now was completely dominant, as he had not only allied himself with Alice Perrers, the reputed mistress of the King, whom she entirely influenced, but had also sought the support of the Pope and the clergy by advising a virtual repeal of the Statute of Provisors by royal prerogative. [21] His actions were viewed with suspicion, and surmises were freely made that he aimed at introducing a Salic law into England, or even at obtaining the throne at the earliest opportunity. Had such a law been passed, no one but the youthful son of the Black Prince would have stood between him and the crown, for Lionel had died in 1368, leaving an only daughter, Philippa, who was married to. Mortimer, Earl of March, by whom she had several sons. So prevalent Were these suspicions that the Parliament of 1376, commonly called the Good Parliament, asked the King to increase his council to ten or twelve peers, without the advice or consent of six of whom, no business should be concluded. The leaders of the party against John of Gaunt, were the Earl of March, William of Wykeham, and Courteney, Bishop of London, who were countenanced, if not actually supported, by the Black Prince. Finding it advisable to propitiate the Lollards, they preferred a long bill against the usurpations of the Pope, but received from the King the answer that he had already provided sufficient remedy. By this action the Papists conciliated the Lollards without losing in any way by it. This being done, Sir Peter de la Mare, Speaker of the House of Commons and Steward to the Earl of

March, boldly impeached the present advisers of the King, who were little more than agents of John of Gaunt. Many of them were convicted of venality and corruption, foremost among them being Lord Latimer and Alice Perrers, [P2] the latter of whom was expressly prohibited, under heavy penalties, from approaching the Court. A new committee of government was formed under the Bishops of London and Winchester which superseded (June 12th) John of Gaunt in his office of negotiator of peace with France. He had been absent all this time from England, but stung by these insults he left Bordeaux, July 8th, determined to reassert his influence. On reaching England he dismissed the committee and recalled Lord Latimer and Alice Perrers, together with his other adherents, who had been banished from the Court Not content with this, be drew up articles of impeachment against Wykeham very similar to those which that prelate had preferred against Lord Latimer. The result was that Wykeham was sentenced to give up the temporalities of Winchester, and not to come within twenty miles of the Court till he had cleared himself of these charges. To obtain popularity John of Gaunt caused the property [Q2] thus confiscated to be given for the time to Richard of Bordeaux, son of the Black Prince, and further installed him as Prince of Wales, declaring him to be the true heir (November 20th), the Black Prince having died June 8th. Owing to that Prince's death he was now undisturbed master of England, but his position was by no means secure owing to the dislike which the people entertained for him. [R2] When the Parliament of 1377 was opened, [S2] he caused a general pardon to be granted to 'all except William of Wykeham — an exception keenly felt by the Bishops in Convocation, who acting under the advice of Courteney, Bishop of London, refused to vote subsidies till Wykeham was restored to his place; their wishes were at last acceded to, and he received a free pardon with the temporalities of Winchester on paying a certain sum of money to the King for the war. So bitter was the resentment of John of Gaunt against Wykeham, that popular rumour felt bound to account for it on other grounds than mere political ones, and it was currently reported [22] that he was not a true son of Edward III., that Philippa had been confined of a daughter who had been exchanged for the son of one of her Gascon attendants, and that he was that son, that Philippa had changed Wykeham on her death-bed to tell the truth as soon as she was dead, a commission which he executed, and thereby incurred the wrath of John of Gaunt.

There does not appear to have been any truth in the story; had it been true, it would have prevented John of Gannt appointing Wykeham one of his trustees in 1373, for Queen Philippa died in 1370, and the story was to have been published immediately on her death.

Wykeham's associates were not overlooked; Sir Peter de la Mare was imprisoned in Nottingham Castle, while the Earl of March was indirectly punished by being ordered to inspect the fortifications of Calais — an office which he declined, as he saw it was given to him to get him out of the way. He consequently resigned the post of Earl Marshal, in which he was succeeded by Lord Percy.

A covert blow was struck by the Bishops in 1377 against John of Gaunt, whose friend Wickliffe was summoned by Convocation to answer certain articles [T2] before his superiors on February 19th, at Saint Paul's.

Wickliffe, who was then a guest at the Savoy, appeared, supported by John of Gaunt and Lord Percy. A spirited war of recrimination was carried on between them and Courteney, Bishop of London, till John of Gaunt was heard to threaten that he would drag the Bishop from his seat by the hair of his head, upon which the assembly broke up in confusion. At this insult to their Bishop, the spirit of the citizens rebelled, and they were roused to action by the conduct of John of Gaunt on the same day, when he proposed to Parliament, through Thomas of Woodstock, that the office of Mayor of London should be abolished, and a custos be appointed as of old, the Earl Marshal having the power of making arrests within the city. [U2] The citizens attacked his palace of the Savoy, and insulted him in every way they could. Fortimately he was dining with a merchant in the city, John de Ypres, and receiving timely warning, fled for refuge by water to the house of the Princess of Wales at Lambeth. [23]

Meanwhile, Bishop Courteney had succeeded in pacifying the rioters, reminding them that it was the holy season of Lent, in which everyone should be especially peaceful Stung by these insults, John of Gaunt caused the mayor and aldermen to be summoned to the King's Palace at Shene, where they were advised to submit to him and to crave his pardon. They declared that they had been quite unable to stop the rage of the mob, but they were superseded in spite of their remonstrances. He was, moreover, able to administer some comfort to himself by procuring from the King a charter, [V2] dated February 28th, granting to the county of Lancaster all the jura regalia which pertain to a County Palatine, as freely as the Earl of Chester enjoyed the same in the county of Chester; while on June 4th, a further charter was granted, giving him the same rights in some lands which he had received in exchange for the Earldom of Richmond, but which had not been specified in the charter dated June 25th, 1372, as he always had in those which were actually mentioned by name. Nor did his various new privileges end here, for on [W2] June 12th, the King issued a licence to him to coin money for two years, in the city of Baion, Castle of Guissen, or in such place as be pleased in the seneschalry of Landerre, of gold, silver, or other metal, and of such coinage, alloy and talc, as he shall think fit, and the profit thereof to accrue to himself.

He had scarcely received this latter charter before Edward III. died, and the crown passed into the feeble bands of Richard of Bordeaux (June 21st), not eleven years old. John of Gaunt had taken every precaution to secure the quiet possession of his nephew, and to absolve himself from the various imputations made on his conduct. He had sent commissioners to Bruges to arrange a truce with France, as peace was of the greatest importance to a young Prince entering on an inheritance straitened and impoverished by a constant drain of men and money. He also arranged Richard's coronation, ordering that everything should be done in the most magnificent manner and with the greatest respect. He himself claimed the office of Hereditary Seneschal of England in right of his Earldom of Leicester; that of Grand Carver in right of his Earldom of Lincoln; and that of Bearer of the Great Sword (curtana) before the King at his coronation in right of his Duchy of Lancaster. His claims to these offices were examined and allowed. On the Thursday before the day of coronation (July 16th), he sat judicially as [X2] Hereditary Seneschal of England, bolding his Court in the Whitehall of the King's Palace at Westminster, where he received the bills and petitions of all those of the nobility and others, as by reason of their tenure or otherwise, claimed to do service at the new King's coronation, and to receive the accustomed fees and allowances. He reconciled himself with the City of London, released De la Mare from prison, and granted an unlimited pardon to Wykeham. These actions, whether extorted from him by the force of circumstances or willingly done, contributed to make the accession of Richard bright and peaceful.

The Parliament would not, however, believe in the innocence of his motives and appointed twelve permanent councillors, without including among them any one of the King's uncles. Finding himself thus mistrusted, he retired to his castle at Kenilworth (that of Hereford his residence, had been recently taken from him) [24] declaring he would have no further share in the government of his country. The first Parliament of Richard II. met on October 13th, and Sir Peter de la Mare was chosen Speaker. The House of Commons invited twelve peers, with "My Lord of Spain" at their head, to confer with them on public affairs. But John of Gaunt begged to be exempted, and complaining bitterly of the reports circulated against him, emphatically declared his innocence of all treasonable thought, and his readiness to maintain his unblemished honour with sword and lance, as though he were the poorest knight in the King's dominions. He further attempted to gain popularity by deserting Alice Perrers, who being brought to trial, had the mortification of finding her old political partner presiding over the court which condemned her. [25]

In the year 1378 he was appointed King's Lieutenant and Captain General for the Dominions of France, with full civil and military power. He received all the money granted for one year by Parliament for the defence of England against France, and sent out several expeditions with varying success. Some ships he had hired at Bayonne defeated a Spanish fleet which was helping the French, in revenge for his laying claim to Castile and Leon, but the Spaniards retaliated by capturing Sir Hugh Courteney and sinking his squadron. John of Gaunt at last set out himself in July, from Southampton, and securing Brest [Y2] with a good garrison, laid siege to St. Malo, but was compelled by Duguesclin to raise it, upon which he returned with his fleet to England. This failure added to his unpopularity, which was further increased by the following event. [26] The Count of Denia, who was taken prisoner at the Battle of Najara by Robert Hawe and John Schakel, had been permitted to return to Spain to procure his ransom, on leaving his son as an hostage. The ransom, however, for some reason or other, was not forthcoming, and the son remained in England. John of Gaunt declared that the young man, being a Castillian, was his subject, and claimed to have the disposal of his person. The captors, refusing to comply with this demand, were sent to the Tower, whence they managed to effect their escape this year (1378), taking refuge in Westminster Abbey.

Here they were attacked during the performance of High Mass by Sir Allan Buxhall, Constable of the Tower, Lord Latimer, and other friends of John of Gaunt. Haide and one of the monks were killed, Schakel being reconfined in the Tower, where he remained till his release in the following year. This gross violation of sanctuary could not pass unnoticed. Courteney, Bishop of London, excommunicated all who were implicated, excepting by name, the King, his mother, and John of Gaunt; this denunciation was made in St. Paul's every Sunday, Wednesday, and Friday. On his return to England John of Gaunt ordered Courteney to desist, and on that prelate declining, summoned him before the Council at Windsor, but the summons was disregarded, and he wisely let the matter drop.

On November 10th he received a charter, [Z2] explaining some general words used in the charter creating the County Palatine of Lancaster, the old charters of July 14th, 1364, June 25th, 1372, June 4th, 1377, having been confirmed by inspeximus, September 15th, 1377.

In this year we find that Robes of the Order of the Garter were provided for the attendance of his wife, Constance of Castile, and his daughters, Philippa and Elizabeth at the feast of St. George. [A3]

In the following year (1379) he received a fresh commission, giving him the largest possible powers beyond seas. [27] The persons who embarked with him on his foreign expeditions were privileged by royal authority, letters of protection being issued by the King, directing that all belonging to the expedition should cross the seas without delay. As De Montfort, who had been the close ally of the English in France, was compelled by his Breton subjects to desert that alliance, the Earl of Buckingham, who was the agent of John of Gaunt, retired with some difficulty. We learn from Walsingham [28] that in the year 1380, a duel took place between Sir John Annesley and Thomas Katrington, the former accusing the latter of treason in selling the Castle of St. Saviour's, in Normandy, to France. On the articles of accusation being read, Katrington took exceptions which were not allowed by John of Gaunt; "quo facto," as Walsingham remarks, "Dux multorum sibi conciliavit gratiam, et partem infamise suae antiquse detersit." What a commentary on the rationale of popularity in those days! Unfortunately, he never seemed to retain it long, and he lost it again by sending an encouraging message to Ralph de Ferrers, who was in prison on a charge of having entered into treasonable correspondence.

It was during this year that he obtained from the King a grant of the marriage of Mary, daughter and co-heiress of Humphrey de Bohun, late Earl of Hereford, valued at 5,000 marks, intending her as a wife for his son, Henry Bolingbroke. [29]

In the autumn of 1380 he proceeded on a commission to Scotland in order to check the ravages which the Scots had committed in Westmoreland and Cumberland, where he remained till the following year, when he signed the "Great Truce," June 18th.

Meanwhile the Parliament had imposed on all persons over fifteen years of age a poll tax [B3] of one shilling per head, the rich to contribute according to their means, it being provided that no one should pay less than one groat, or more than sixty. The tax was hateful enough to the people in itself, but when a brutal system of collection was added, the long-suffering commons could endure it no longer, and a fearful insurrection broke out in Kent and the Eastern Counties, under the leadership of Wat Tyler and Jack Straw. After committing various enormities on their way to London, they proceeded to attack the capital, and marching, or rather rioting through the streets, did an immense damage both to life and property. John of Gaunt's palace, the Savoy, [C3] was a special object of their vengeance; they completely destroyed it, burning it to the ground, June 13th. They also used every device they could think of for insulting him: for instance, they put some of his valuable dresses on poles, to be shot at by arrows, and afterwards destroyed them with their swords, [30] declaring no King of England should ever be called John. To show that this destruction was wrought out of hatred to John of Gaunt, and not for the sake of plunder, they carried nothing away with them, but let the fire consume all. The death of Wat Tyler [D3] and the firmness of the King quelled the insurrection, which had at one time assumed such formidable proportions. William Walworth, who slew Wat Tyler, and three other citizens, were made knights, affording the first instances in which the insignia of chivalry were thus diverted from their original appropriation. The title of "Lord" was at the same time annexed to the dignity of Mayor, a dagger being also added to the city arms out of compliment to Walworth's gallantry. Great consternation was felt in John of Gaunt's palace at Leicester, where his wife Constance was residing, when the news of the burning of the Savoy reached that town. She fled to Knaresborough, after having been refused admittance at Pontefract, the governor of that place fearing her presence might induce an attack upon him. All the valuables in the palace were hurriedly removed to Saint Mary's Church, Leicester, in hopes that the sanctity of the place might protect them. Nor were these precautions unnecessary, for the palace did not escape pillage -from the hands of insurgents.

This insurrection so interrupted the proceedings of the Courts of Justice at Westminster, that the King issued a proclamation to John of Gaunt, ordaining that, owing to the unheard commotions in England, all the pleadings in the Court of King's Bench, stood adjourned, and that all writs and mandates delivered to John of Gaunt or his ministers within the County of Lancaster, should be returned on October 7th, 1381, instead of the usual time. [31] Sinister rumours were abroad that he had secretly fomented these disturbances, [E3] and it had to be officially declared that he had always been faithful to the Crown. [32]

While all these disturbances were taking place in England, he was absent on the King's service in Scotland, where he signed a treaty on June 18th. As he returned he was refused admittance at Berwick, and was consequently induced to accept an offer of hospitality made to him by the nobles of Scotland. He remained for some time their guest at Edinburgh, and a report got abroad that he wished to make use of the Scots to obtain the English Throne. It is true they had offered, in the noble spirit of chivalry, to escort him safely through England and help him to redress his grievances, but it is equally true he had declined their assistance, [33] It is, however, by no means impossible that Richard II.'s friendly letter to him of July 6th, was written under fear of his arriving, backed up by such powerful allies. At any rate for some reason or other Richard's conduct towards him underwent a sudden change, which resulted in this letter and an order for the various high officials of each county to give him a large escort on his way from Scotland. He probably returned about the middle of August, [F3] though there is no *certain* indication of his presence in England till November, when we find him proposing in Parliament to transport 2,000 men and 2,000 archers to Spain if the House would enable him to raise £60,000 (equivalent to £1,000,000 of modem money), engaging himself to repay it by good securities. He made a similar proposal in the autumn of 1382, but on neither occasion was he successful. He was, however, able to procure a grant from the King, giving him license to coin gold and silver by Pelegrin de Ler for two years, to date from August 1380, on the same terms as before. He had received early this year (1381) an invitation from the King of Portugal to come over with Edmund, and make an attempt on Castile, the said King promising not only his assistance, but also his daughter and heiress, in marriage to Edmund's son. Edmund accepted the offer and crossed over to Spain, but John of Gaunt, being in Scotland, was unable to go, [G3] which gave such offence to the King of Portugal that he made peace with Spain, and Edmund was forced to return to England.

Stow says, that John of Gaunt gave as reasons for the expedition, that the King of Portugal "might thereby be bound to aide the King of England, and stop the passage of the straites of Gibraltare or of Moroc from the galleis that must of necessitie passe by the same straites to come to infest the British or English ocean, for so should England be safe and France should be deceived." This was perhaps the only reason that would weigh with Parliament, who would not feel in any way bound or inclined to forward his claims to the throne of Castile.

Parliament was considerably disturbed this autumn by quarrels between him and Northumberland, arising out of the latter refusing him admittance at Berwick. The King, however, took the blame upon himself and was able to reconcile them at least outwardly.

The spring of the year 1382 was marked by Archbishop Courteney convening a Synod at the Grey Friars, in London, for the purpose of deliberating on measures to be taken against Wickliffe. [34] They determined to 1382. call upon him to answer on one doctrine alone — that of the Eucharist. This was a matter purely spiritual, and so crucial a point that many persons, who were willing enough to support him in his crusade against the wealth and arrogance of the clergy, shrank from joining him in impugning it. Among these was John of Gaunt; on being appealed to by Wickliffe, he advised him to withdraw from such stormy fights, and to avow publicly his submission to his ecclesiastical superiors. [H3] He did not mean to separate himself completely from the Lollards, for we find him saving Dr. Hereford and William de Swinderby from being put to death for holding these principles.

In connection with this he issued a proclamation [I3] to the sheriffs of the County of Lancaster, ordaining that the "Holy Anglican Mother Church" should have all its liberties whole and unimpaired, and fully enjoy the same; which would rather make us suppose that he wished to remove from himself all suspicion of being a Lollard.

After renewing the Scotch treaty of 1381, he was appointed Richard's lieutenant for the kingdom of France, with powers scarcely less than royal. [35] Previous to his appointment the Bishop of Norwich had been sent to the assistance of the free burghers of Ghent, hut had retreated ignominiously before the armies of Flanders and France. The ill success of this expedition was attributed in England to the jealousy of John of Gaunt, who was accused of thwarting it in every way he could, though the charge seems unfounded. It probably arose from the fact that the Bishop of Norwich and John of Gaunt had presented rival schemes to Parliament at the same time, and that the Parliament had accepted the Bishop's by preference.

He went to France to conclude a treaty shortly before Christmas [36] and returned early in the year 1384, only to proceed immediately to the North to repress the Scotch inroads, in which he met with only moderate success. [J3] A result of his expedition was an agreement between him and Northumberland, that the Freemen of Lancaster and Durham were ta assemble by order of their lord, and to come with all their power, whenever Northumberland made proclamation that the Scots had laid siege to any King's castle. While he was thus absent a conspiracy was formed against him at Court by the King's favourites, who were naturally anxious to rid themselves of so powerful a rival, and Sir Robert Tresilian, Lord Chief Justice of the {Ling's Bench, was the legal tool to be employed to crush him. Their animus against him was strongly shown at the election of the Lord Mayor of London, for which office there were two candidates. John of Northampton, the popular candidate, famous for his edicts against usury, was countenanced by John of Gaunt; but the election of his opponent. Sir Nicholas Brembar, was secured by military interference, while the former was imprisoned first in Corfe Castle and then in Carisbrooke. Parliament met April 20th, soon after John of Gaunt's return from Scotland, and early in the Session, John Latimer, a Carmelite Friar, presented a schedule [37] to the King, accusing the Duke of a design to murder the King and usurp the throne. The King communicated the tale to two of his chaplains, and during the conversation, John of Gaunt entered the room. [38] Finding himself very coldly received, he thought they were talking of him and retired. The chaplains strongly advised the King to tell him everything. Their advice was taken, and, on hearing the accusation, he emphatically protested his entire innocence of the charges brought against him, and demanded that his accuser should be arrested. Having convinced the King of his integrity, his request was granted, and Latimer was placed in the custody of Sir John Holland, who had married the Duke's eldest daughter. Latimer died in his prison with every appearance of foul play; indeed, there can be no doubt but that he fell a victim to the Lancastrian party, who were afraid some unpleasant revelations might be made about their chief. It was to him that the imputation of guilt naturally clung, nor could he persuade the people that he had no hand in the murder.

At the beginning of August he crossed over to France, where his negotiations resulted in the truce being extended to the following spring. With their usual cowardice his enemies took advantage of his absence to prosecute one of his friends, John of Northampton, who complained that his trial "ought not to passe in the absence of his Lord the Duke of Lancaster." This remonstance was of no avail; he was condemned to perpetual imprisonment, while his goods were confiscated to the use of the Crown.

The conspiracy against John of Gaunt was ripening fast; a special commission was given to Tresilian to try any accusation it might be thought proper to prefer against him, but he received intelligence of it before the project was quite ready, and withdrew quietly to Pontefract, which he carefully fortified. The state of affairs' seemed so critical to the Princess of Wales that she came out of her retirement to effect a reconciliation between him and the King. [39]

In spite of failing health and bodily infirmity, she undertook a long journey to achieve her purpose, in which she proved quite successful; Bo that we find Richard signifying by writ, dated June

13th, [40] to John of Gaunt, that for the welfare of his Crown and kingdom, and the suppression of his enemies, the Scots, he purposed being at Newcastle, July 14th, and commanded his uncle to be there. In obedience to these orders, he joined the King, who, forcing the Scots to retreat from Northumberland, traversed Scotland with 80,000 men, and burnt Edinburgh and Aberdeen, as well as other towns. But the Scots, together with their French allies, under the Lord High Admiral de Vienne, meanwhile marched into Cumberland, compelling Richard to leave Scotland, in order to prevent their ravages. As soon as he came they retreated, boasting they had done as much harm in England as he had in Scotland; indeed the armies themselves never came to blows. [41] At Edinburgh, Richard had a most violent quarrel with John of Gaunt, refusing in any way to listen to him, or take his advice; this conduct is usually ascribed to the insinuations of the Chancellor, Michael de la Pole, one of Richard's favourites. It had the effect of convincing the King's uncles that he could not be depended upon, and though he tried to conciliate his younger uncles by creating Thomas, Duke of Gloucester, and Edmund, Duke of York, the feeling of mistrust never left them. It also probably hastened the departure of John of Gaunt for Spain, as his position in England became unpleasant, if not actually unsafe. He sailed from Plymouth, [K3] on July 8th, 1386, with a force of 20,000 men, [L3] Sir Thomas Percy being his Admiral of the Fleet, and Sir John Holland, Constable of his forces. Before his departure, Richard and his "good Queen Anne" gave respectively to himself and his wife a crown of gold, ordering that all should acknowledge them as King and Queen of Castile and Leon. Many Castillians regarded his wife's claim to that throne as sacred, while the King of Portugal was eager to obtain English help against the reigning King of Castile — the son of Enrique of Transtamare — who laid claim to Portugal, and was now actually besieging the capital.

    The opportunity consequently seemed an unusually favourable one for making the attempt to win the throne he so much coveted He landed at Corunna on August 9th, having spent three days of his voyage in an unsuccessful attack on Brest. His first campaign in Spain was marked by victory, many towns capitulating, and the Spaniards giving way before him everywhere; but in the second, his army was almost annihilated by disease and famine. [M3] This, in conjunction with his own failing health, compelled him to retreat to that part of Aquitaine, which still remained to the English, where he spent the winter of 1387. Richard took advantage of his presence there, to issue a new commission to him as lieutenant in those parts, [42] and soon after granted him the fief of the Duchy of Aquitaine, in the same way as the Black Prince had enjoyed it. [43] [N3] Circumstances, however, enabled him to conclude a highly advantageous treaty with his adversary, the reigning King of Castile. In 1388 he opened negotiations with France, with a view to marrying Catherine, his daughter by Constance, to the Duc de Bern, uncle of the King of France. The idea of having the claim to his throne in such hands was so repugnant to John of Castile, that he used every means in his power to prevent the match taking place. In this he succeeded, for by the most alluring overtures he induced John of Gaunt to consent to a marriage between Catherine and Enrique of Asturias, his son. By the treaty made between John of Gaunt and John of Castile, the former resigned all claims to the throne on receiving 200,000 nobles (£1,200,000 of modern money,) as an indemnity for his expenses, and a pension of £10,000 per annum on himself and his wife respectively. [O3] As he had previously married Philippa, his eldest daughter by Blanche, to John, King of Portugal, he succeeded in entailing the Crowns of Portugal and Spain on his descendants. No reasonable man could have expected such a successful termination to his expedition, considering the enormous difficulties it presented, and John of Gaunt might well congratulate himself on what he had managed to achieve. He returned to England in November, 1389, in time to attend a great council of peers, which was then sitting at Beading, and to spend his Christmas at Hertford. He found the King and Gloucester at open feud, and it was only with considerable difficulty that he managed to effect a reconciliation between them. During his absence, Gloucester, making himself master of England, had compelled the King to acquiesce in whatever he did, nor was it till the beginning of 1389 that the King was able to re-assert his authority, which he did by one of those happy flashes of genius that were not entirely foreign to his character. Naturally he was unwilling to be very friendly with his uncle after such treatment, and we can feel no surprise at it rankling in his mind.

In 1390, we find (May 20th) John of Gaunt named [44] as one of the peers who complained to the Pope of the exorbitances and encroachments of the Apostolical See. Earlier in the year he received a new charter [45] reciting the charters of February 28th, 1377, and November 10th, 1378, and extending them to the heirs male of his body, with the proviso that the title of Duke of Lancaster should be retained. The only other mention of him this year is by Knighton, [46] who informs us that he held a great hunting in Leicester forest, at which the King and Queen were both present.

In the following year he received a grant, [47] exempting him during his life from paying any fees for the Great Seal, or any other Seals, for any letters patent, commissions, writs, or judgments, in any of the King's Courts.

On being commissioned in 1392 to treat with France about peace, he went over to Amiens, where he received a most magnificent welcome, the King with all his great nobles coming out to meet him. He concluded a truce for one year and then returned to England, his expenses to and from Calais being defrayed by France. [48]

In 1393, he and his brother Thomas complained to the King that Sir Thomas Talbot, with his adherents, was conspiring their deaths in divers parts of Cheshire, as was confessed and well known; they therefore prayed the interference of Parliament, which being granted, resulted in Sir Thomas being adjudged guilty of high treason. The next year, several chaises were made against him in the House of Lords, by Lord Arundel, who afterwards not only retracted his words, but made him a public apology. [49]

Having received a commission in 1394, [50] as lieutenant in Picardy, he was deputed with Thomas to negotiate a renewal of the French truce. With this object in view, he crossed over in May, to Lenlyngham, between Calais and Boulogne, where he was successful in extending the truce over a further period of four years. Soon after his return his wife Constance died (July) and was buried at Leicester.

In 1395, he went to Aquitaine to take possession of the Duchy, but the inhabitants declined to recognize him, except as King's lieutenant, refusing to be separated from the Crown of England. On an appeal to the King it was decreed that Aquitaine should always remain in the demesne of the Crown; still it does not appear that the grant was actually withdrawn from him. [51] He returned to England about Michaelmas, and in the following January married Catherine Swinford, who for some time past had been his mistress. [P3] By this marriage he became brother-in-law of Chaucer, the poet, with whom he had always been on terms of the greatest intimacy, but whom he now loaded with still greater favours, presenting him among other things with the valuable estate of Donnington Castle.

There is an absurd story related by Leland and Sandford of his moving in Parliament about this time that his son Henry be declared heir to the Crown, saying that the first Earl of Lancaster was really the elder brother of Edward I., but had been put aside owing to personal deformity, whence he received the name Crouchback. There is no foundation for this story, which would appear to be a coinage of the supporters of Henry IV. in their eager desire to make him out to be the legitimate king. There is hardly any necessity to add that the term "Crouchback" really refers to the cross worn at the backs of those who had taken the vow of pilgrimage or Crusade to the Holy Land, as for instance, the Crossed or Crutched Friars. [52]

Early in 1396, Richard, attended by John of Gaunt and Thomas, crossed over to Calais, [53] to meet the King of France, but they returned after a brief interview, leaving their wives behind. In the beginning of October they rejoined them, and John of Gaunt, with his wife and his son Henry, accompanied Thomas to Saint Omers for a conference with the Dukes of Burgundy and Brittany. On his return to Calais, he proceeded with Richard to Guisnes, where they met the King of France. Visits of ceremony were interchanged, and the two Kings dined together, Richard being waited on by John of Gaunt and Thomas, Charles VI. by two peers of the French royal blood. The Kings parted at the end of October, and Richard with his uncles reached London early in November. [54]

The result of this journey was a marriage between Richard and Isabella of France, then only seven years old, and a thirty years truce. Thomas was very angry about the match, opposing it with unsuccessful vigour, as he considered it would induce a real peace between England and France, and strengthen the King's hands. He confided his views to the Duke of York "for he was but a soft prince; but to the Duke of Lancaster, his eldest brother, he durst not speak over largely for he saw well that he was of the King's opinion, and was well pleased with the King's marriage." [55]

On June 29th, John of Gaunt received a [Q3] confirmation of certain charters by inspeximus, several additional privileges being also granted to him, while early in 1397, he obtained an Act of Parliament, legitimating [56] the children Lady Swinford had borne to him previously, the eldest of whom was now created Earl of Somerset, the second one being elected Bishop of Lincoln in the following year. Another concession made to him was permission to import sixty casks of wine, duty free, for household use; this was a grant of some value, as the duty was 3s. per cask, with an *ad valorem* duty of 5 per cent, on introduction into the port of London. These are usually held to have been [57] bribes to induce him to support the Court, which was very much in need of assistance, as great discontent prevailed about the French marriage. A dangerous conspiracy was being formed, the chief actors in which were Thomas of Woodstock, the Archbishop of Canterbury, and the Earls of Arundel and Warwick. Richard managed to forestall them, and they were all taken into custody. The three latter on being brought to trial were condemned, Lord Arundel to be executed, the others to be kept in perpetual imprisonment. John of Gaunt, as Hereditary Great Steward of England, presided at their trial, and by so doing gave a sanction to the proceedings of the Government. Thomas of Woodstock was never tried, but was transported to Calais; the governor, on being asked to produce him for trial, answered that he had suddenly died in custody. [R3] There can be but little doubt that he was secretly murdered by order of the King, who was afraid to bring him to trial on account of his popularity. He perhaps feared meeting the same fate as Edward XL, who, soon after beheading Thomas, Earl of Lancaster, first Prince of the blood, was deposed.

A great quarrel broke out in January, 1398, between Henry of Bolingbroke, who had just been created Duke of Hereford, John of Gaunt's eldest son, and Thomas Mowbray, Duke of Norfolk, the governor of Calais, under whose care Thomas of Woodstock had been placed. Bolingbroke accused Mowbray of inciting him to sedition, [S3] and the two were ordered to decide their quarrel at Coventry with sword and lance. Everyone knows how Richard interfered, sentencing Bolingbroke to banishment for six years, Mowbray for life. It is said that John of Gaunt consented, if he did not actually advise, to have this sentence passed on his son.

He had previously been commissioned [58] to amend and reform all matters contrary to the truces with France and Scotland, but before he was able to finish this work he died at Ely House, Holborn, in the fifty-ninth year of his age. (Feb. 3rd, 1399.) The Monkish historians of this period attempt to cast a slur on his character, by asserting that he died of a loathsome disease, contracted by his immoral way of living. [T3]

It is a favourite habit of men to represent their enemies as dying a shameful death, or by the visitation of God. For instance, Capgrave [59] says of Wickliffe — "And worthily was he smet on Seynt Thomas day, ageyn whom he had gretely offendid, letting men of that pilgrimage, and conveniently deid he in Silvestir fest, ageyn whom he had venemously berkid for dotacion of the Church." There is no reason to suppose that this is anything but a calumny on John of Gaunt, and entirely unfounded. It is by no means impossible that he really died of a disease contracted from exposure in Spain, in the same way as the Black Prince. He was with that Prince on the deadly plains of Valladolid, in 1367, and though we have no account of any suffering on his part, still he could hardly have escaped altogether. We know for certain, however, that his health was very much injured in his Spanish campaign of 1387, [U3] and his comparative retirement from active life after his return to England, rather points to the conclusion that he was ever afterwards in failing health.

He was buried under the pavement of the Church of St. Paul's, by the side of his first wife, Blanche, and a stately tomb [60] was erected to him and his second wife Constance, who had been laid in the Collegiate Church of Our Lady, at Leicester. A special order from the Court alone saved it from destruction during the general demolition of altars and shrines, in the fourth year of Queen Elizabeth; it was saved, however, only for a time, for it was unfortunately destroyed in 1666 by the Great Fire of London.

It was, as is well known, the universal belief of this period that masses for the dead had the effect of shortening the time the departed had to endure the pains of Purgatory. The friends of those who had died naturally saw to the performance of such services as might benefit the dead. There was a simple form [61] which was usually resorted to — viz., that of the obit, or anniversary of the death, performed by the ordinary priests attached to the church, on some special day. A copy [62] of the Statutes of St. Paul's, transcribed by the authority of Dean Lyseux, in 1440, shows that obits were performed on February 2nd for John of Gaunt, and on September 12th, for his wife Blanche.

The more ambitious and costly form was to build chantries, where masses were to be sung for ever for the repose of the souls of the departed. Henry IV., soon after his accession, granted a license for a chantry in St. Paul's, opposite to his father's tomb. Also for one in the Collegiate Church of our Lady at Leicester, called the New Work, for the good estate of the said King, during his life in this world, and afterwards for the health of his soul, and the souls of his father and mother, and for the soul of the Lady Constance, former wife to John of Gaunt, whose body lieth interred in the same 'Collegiate Church. The executors of John of Gaunt were also permitted to purchase lands to the value of £40 (rather more than £600 of modem money) per annum to support these two chantries, and keep the anniversaries of their deaths, of him and his wife Blanche. In the tenth year of his reign, Henry IV. gave to St. Paul's divers messuages and lands within the City of London, for the anniversaries of John of Gaunt and Blanche yearly in the same cathedral, with Placebo and Dirige, 19 antiphons, 19 psalms, 19 lessons in the exequies of each; also Mass of Requiem, with Note on the Morrow to be performed at the High Altar for ever, and to distribute to the Dean (when present) 3*s.* 4*d.*, petty canons 10*s.*, chaplains 20*s.*, vicars 6*s.* 8*d.*, choristers 2*s.* 6*d.* vergers 1*s.*, bell-ringers 6*d.*, keepers of lamps about the tomb, at each anniversary, 6*d.*, the mayor 3*s.* 4*d.*, the sheriffs (when present) 3*s.* 4*d.*, Bishop of London as rent of the house where the chantry priests resided, 10*s.* The Dean and Chapter were to provide eight great tapers to bum at the tomb on the days of the anniversaries, at the exequies, and Mass on the Morrow; also at the Processions, Masses, Vespers, on any great Festival, and on Sundays at the Procession, Mass and second Vespers for ever. They were further ordered to provide for those priests belonging to the chapel on the north part of the tomb, a certain chalice, missal and portvoise, according to the Ordinale Sarum, vestments, bread, wine, wax, and glasses, will all other ornaments necessary for the same. All these expenses, together with the repairs of the house, were to be defrayed from the rent of the lands given by the King.

John of Gaunt had provided by his will for two chaplains, who were to perform daily service for ever for the repose of his soul and that of his wife Blanche. He further directed that on the day of his burial there should be burnt "ten tapers in the name of the ten commandments, which I have transgressed too wickedly; seven tapers in memory of the seven works of charity I neglected, and the seven deadly sins; five tapers in honour of the five principal wounds of Christ, and the five senses which I have very negligently wasted, for which I pray God's mercy, and three tapers in honour of the Trinity." His body was to be kept forty days, on each of which forty silver marks were to be distributed to the poor, with an additional 300 on the eve of his burial. Such were the final wishes of John of Gaunt.

[1] Cart, in Officina Ducatûs Lancastriae.
[2] Barnes, ii. 14, § 20.
[3] Rymer, v. 833. (30 Edw. III., Jan. 20, 1356.)
[4] Walsingham, i. 286.
[5] Rymer, vi. 178-196. (34 Edw. III., May 8th, 1360.)
[6] Walsingham, p. 294, "Astante Rege cum filiis suis."
[7] Sandford, Book i., chap. iv. Genealogical History of England.
[8] Rymer, vi., 384-390. (July 19th, 1362. 36 Edw. III.)
[9] Cf. Stow. ad. ann. 1396.
[10] Barne's Hist, of Edward III., p. 675.
[11] Histoire Duguesclin.
[12] Froissart, vol. i., c. 233.
[13] Froissart, vol. i., c. 238-9.
[14] Rymer, vi., 621. (June 3rd, 1369. 43 Edw. III.)
[15] Circa festum Nativitatis Beatae Mariae (Sept. 8).— Walsingham i., 307.
[16] Rot. Vascon, 43 Edw. III., m. 5. Turr, Lond.
[17] Lowth, Life of Wykeham, p. 61.
[18] Froissart, vol. i., c. 295.
[19] Rymer, VII., 83-87. (Sep. 1, 1375. 49Edw. III.)
[20] Lowth's Wykeham, 63. Hook's Lives of the Archbishops of Canterbury, iv., 239.
[21] Hook's Lives of the Archbishops of Canterbury, iv., 256.
[22] Monk of Evesham, Anglia Sacra i., 318. Fasciculi Zizaniorum (Rolls' Collection), p. xxv., intro.
[23] Collins, p. 25.
[24] Collin's Life of John of Gaunt.
[25] Lowth's Life of Wykeham, 154, note.
[26] Walsingham, i., 375.
[27] Rymer, vii, 218. (June 12th, 1379. 2 Rich. II.)
[28] Walsingham, i., 430.
[29] Collins, p. 40.
[30] Walsingham, i., 457.
[31] Claus.4 Rich. II., m. I.

[32] Pat, 5 Rich. II., m. 1, July 3.
[33] Walsingham, ii., 42.
[34] Milman's Hist. Lat. Christ, vii., 127.
[35] Rymer vii., 408-410. (7 Rich. II., Sept. 12, 1383.)
[36] Stow ad. ann.
[37] Rymer vii., 425. (April 23rd, 1384. 7 Rich. II.)
[38] History of the Civil Wars of England, between the two Houses of Lancaster and York. By Sir Francis Biondi, translated from the Italian by, Earle of Monmouth (A.D 1641), p. 4. Godwin's account is somewhat different.
[39] Walsingham ii., 126.
[40] Rymer vii., 474. (June 13th, 1386. 8 Rich. II.)
[41] Walsingham ii., 132.
[42] Rymer vii., 586. (May 30th, 1388. 11 Rich. II.)
[43] Rymer vii., 659. (March 2nd, 1389. 12 Rich. II.)
[44] Rymer vii., 672. (May 26th, 1390. 13 Rich. II.)
[45] Feb. 16th, 1390, Charters of the Duchy of Lancaster.
[46] Knighton, p. 2737.
[47] Rymer vii., 695. (Feb. 8th, 1391. 14 Rich. II.)
[48] Walsingham ii., 205.
[49] Pet. 17, rec. 2, m. 15.
[50] Feb. 22nd, 1394.
[51] Cf. Note 67.
[52] Pennant, London, p. 347.
[53] Collins' Life of John of Gaunt, p. 68.
[54] Stow says "before Allhallowne day," p. 506.
[55] Slow ad. Ac.
[56] Cf. Excerpta Historica (Lond., 1831), p. 152.
[57] Hook. Lives of Arch. Canterbury, iv., 435.
[58] Rymer viii., 32.
[59] Capgrave, p. 240.
[60] Milman's Hist. S. Paul's, 81, 375, with Dugdale's engraving of the tomb.
[61] Dugdale, p. 356.
[62] It is in the Camb. University Library. Milman's Hist. S. Paul's, 515.

# Chapter Two - Character and Influence of John of Gaunt

It is a considerable misfortune for the proper estimation of the position of the various English statesmen of this century that the names of Edward III. and the Black Prince ore gilded with such overwhelming lustre. They stand out in so strong a relief, that all others seem to us small and insignificant beside them; nor is it easy to draw the veil which has so shrouded them in the history of romance that they appear almost beings of a different mould to ourselves. Their overshadowing reputation has completely eclipsed that of many who would otherwise have been regarded as of the first rank, and whose names would have been handed down to posterity. Still there remain a few who have not sunk into oblivion, amongst whom is John of Gaunt, and even he is chiefly remembered now as a supporter of Wickliffe in his conflicts with the Church. Far from being the ablest of the statesmen who surrounded the English throne, he owed most of his influence and power to the enormous wealth which he acquired by his marriage with his cousin Blanche, the heiress of Henry, Duke of Lancaster. He was, moreover, always the favourite son of Edward III., his father, whose partiality to him was shown on many occasions. These advantages, combined with the weak state of health of the Black Prince, enabled him practically to rule England as he pleased during the last few years of his father's reign. His dictatorship, for his tenure of power almost amounted to that, was marked by the successful temporary settlement of the great clergy question, which had been agitating England for some years. This, in itself, was no mean thing to boast of, especially as he diplomatically permitted the Pope to levy a large sum of money from the English ecclesiastics. It may be doubted, whether his hatred of the clergy did not here outrun his discretion, for it is always questionable policy to crush your enemies by permitting another power to aggrandize itself at their expense. He was certainly, for the time, reversing the policy of Edward I., who had strictly forbidden the exportation of ecclesiastical revenues from the kingdom. Still, it was very desirable to weaken the power of the Church, and to enable the laity to assert their rights, which had been grievously encroached upon. Had he been actuated by motives of pure patriotism, he would have deserved unqualified praise, but I think his reasons were very different. Godwin has tried to show that he never meant to usurp the throne, nor in any way to dispossess the King. Now I agree with this so far that I feel sure Shakespeare is right when he represents John of Gaunt saying he would never lift his hand against the King; [V3] but rebelling and claiming a vacant throne are two very distinct things. It seems to me that in his ambition he longed to sit on the English throne, and would have sought his way to it by any means not absolutely illegitimate. He was loyal to the extent of not plotting against the reigning

King, but no further. He wished to exclude the children of his niece Philippa from the Crown, by introducing a Salic law into England. Had he made the attempt, and succeeded in it, Richard of Bordeaux would have been the only person between him and the Crown. The chances would then have been highly favourable for his succession, and, indeed, as events turned out, certain. Now the clergy were a very powerful body, desirous of peace, and of keeping the sovereignty in the right line for the present. They must either be conciliated or crushed, but which) The English people were no admirers of the dissolute monks, and would gladly take an opportunity of injuring them; while the Pope was willing to enrich himself at their expense, without caring much, so long as his power was not questioned. In the end, John of Gaunt determined to crush the clergy, and in 1371, as I have shown, caused a petition to be presented to the King, begging him to supersede his ecclesiastical ministry by laymen. To further his views, he made common cause for some time with Wickliffe, though actuated by very different motives. [W3] The Pope, meanwhile, was propitiated by an offer to obtain from the King a virtual repeal of the Statute of Provisors. The clergy did not view these actions with indifference, but aimed a blow at John of Gaunt by summoning Wickliffe to appear at St. Paul's, thus indirectly attacking his patron.

I am also inclined to think that his claim to the throne of Castile was made with a view to further his wishes relative to the English Crown. He assumed the insignia of King of Castile in 1371, but made no attempt to sustain his pretensions till 1386 — a lapse of fifteen years. He could have had several opportunities to invade Spain, during that time, had he pleased, and there must have been some reason for his remaining content with an empty honour so long. Why may it not have been that he called himself King of Castile with a view to accustoming people to speak and hear of him as one enjoying royal rank? Had he become King of England, they would have been quite used to calling him King, and the position would seem more natural. Thus his attack on the clergy, his conciliation of the Pope, his wishes for a Salic law, his assumption of the title of King, all were part of a vast scheme to secure the throne of England legitimately, and with the consent and support of the people. Failing this, he would be content with that of Castile, and so we find in 1386, less than four years after Richard's marriage, when there was little hope of his attaining his object in England, he sailed to Spain to prosecute his claim there. Unable to succeed for himself, he was gratified by seeing his daughters seated on the thrones of Castile and Portugal.

To carry out this comprehensive scheme with any degree of success, would have required a cold and wary politician, but the qualities of John of Gaunt were essentially the reverse. He never could make himself really popular, for all good impressions of him were speedily removed by some intemperate action or burst of ungovernable anger. His want of skill in concealing his designs, so as to remove the people's suspicions, his deliberate insult to the Bishop of London at St. Paul's, his participation in the murder of John Latimer his acquiescence in that of Thomas of Woodstock, his permitting the sanctuary at Westminster to be violated, testify alike to his want of self-control, and to the waywardness of his nature. This was the greatest bane of his life, and prevented him being of the use he ought to have been to his country, by losing him the confidence of the people. Everything he did was received with suspicion, nor could all his protestations of innocence change the popular feeling which was strongly shown in the insurrection of 1381. After this he became very unpopular at Court, owing to his openly evincing his dislike of the favourites who surrounded the King. His position, consequently, was so insecure, that he was glad to absent himself &om England, and the King was equally pleased to get rid of his powerful uncle.

During the last years of his life he kept aloof from domestic politics as much as possible, though occasionally occupying himself with the foreign affairs of the nation.

It is extremely difficult to unravel the political intrigues of Richard's reign. Not only were they numerous and intricate, but there was such universal mistrust prevailing, that courtiers did not feel it prudent to commit themselves entirely to one party, and the confusion became terrible. In all this entanglement, John of Gaunt was more sinned against than sinning, for he was unequal to carrying out conspiracies with success. As has been seen, such a slow form of attaining his end was not in accordance with his nature. He preferred, like an old feudal baron, to pursue a rough and ready way of gratifying his wishes, and was too impatient to wait to employ more legitimate means. Had he but possessed the confidence of the people, he would have been able to have swayed the Councils of the State for many years; but when the Court became hostile to him, he had nothing to fall back upon, and was almost compelled to quit the country for a time. Where his own interests were not much concerned, he was always willing to promote those of England, and he took considerable pains to preserve peace as much as possible between England and France after his hopes of obtaining the English Crown were overthrown.

During the French wars, he was a brave but unsuccessful commander, distinguishing himself by his courage rather than by his skill. The history of these wars is incomplete, and little is known of them save the leading events, and their results, so that it is hard to fathom the ability of the various commanders. Success was then the measure of skill, but the reputation of leaders was also largely based on their bravery and knightly conduct, apart from all other considerations. [X3]

It is a sufficient commentary on his generalship to observe that his name is never associated with those of distinguished English soldiers.

Besides his connection with the State Councils of England, he was lord paramount of the County Palatine of Lancaster, and this county seems to have grievously suffered by his continual absence and care for other matters. The immorality existing in this county became so deplorable that he was forced to issue a stringent proclamation on the subject, but so far as we know, he took no pains to suppress the real source of this evil — viz., the Maintainers. These banditti, composed of the scum of the disbanded armies of Edward III., levied blackmail, plundered villages, and committed all kinds of excesses in the Counties Palatine of Cheshire and Lancashire, where they principally established themselves. It is true they existed in other parts of England, but not.', in so great a force; nor were they guilty of such enormities elsewhere.

The government of these counties was shamefully neglected, and complaints were rife that it was useless to pay heavy taxes when it was uncertain whether law and order would be ensured. Much of this was doubtless owing to the insufficiency of subordinates, but this can only partly excuse the neglect with which he appears to have treated his more immediate dependents.

He was in reality a good specimen of an old English baron, ambitious, unaccustomed to self-restraint, and too apt to substitute might for right. He was never fitted to take part in Court intrigues, or in anything that required real tact and discernment. Still there is one important point in which he was far beyond his age, and that is his enlightened patronage of learned men. Among his most intimate friends was the poet Chaucer, who has taken so prominent a position in the annals of English literature. The extent of the intimacy is clearly shown in the poems of Chaucer, some of which deal with events in the life of John of Gaunt in a way that proves the close friendship existing between them. Several offices of importance were conferred on Chaucer, so as to afford not merely independent but handsome means; and, when his patron became his brother-in-law, he received the valuable estate of Donnington Castle.

Wickliffe, too, experienced the favours of John of Gaunt, who was originally attracted to him by his great knowledge and learning. No doubt in after days he found the stem reformer a most wonderful ally in his attack upon the Church, but still the reasons that first cemented their friendship were entirely literary. His refusal to support Wickliffe in his denial of the truth of the doctrine of Transubstantiation brought about a coolness between them, which seems never to have been really removed, though this was doubtless owing in part to the secluded life led by the reformer for the four years between the controversy of the Real Presence and his death.

Another instance of his love for the society of able scholars is afforded in the person of the Bishop of Limoges, whom he saved from the violent death which the Black Prince had destined for him, as a proper punishment for his treachery. That the Bishop thoroughly deserved to die is beyond question: he had been loaded with the greatest favours by the Black Prince, and he requited all this by an act of the grossest treachery. Still he was a man of vast erudition, and this saved his life by securing him the patronage of John of Gaunt, who induced the Pope to intercede for him.

William of Wykeham received several proofs of John of Gaunt's confidence and regard, though during the latter end of their lives, political rivalry unfortunately begot private enmity. Immeasurably inferior to Wykeham in statesmanship and learning, he was yet a formidable antagonist by mere force of his position as a royal Duke of enormous wealth. Had he not possessed these advantages, the temptation to cope with Wykeham might never have occurred to him, except as an idle dream never to be realized, and their friendship would have remained unbroken. The patriotic spirit of Wykeham could not brook the ambitious and unconstitutional tendencies of his friend, and a separation ensued, which was never healed up.

There is no evidence to show that John of Gaunt extended his patronage to commercial interests more conspicuously than the other Princes of royal blood. H«, as well as they, was an honorary member of the Merchant Taylors' Company, which shows the estimation in which mercantile affairs were now held; but there is no special mention of his doing anything more than the other Princes.

Let us now turn to the mare private part of his life of his three marriages, the first and third were prompted by feelings of affection, the second by those of ambition. Chaucer in his "Dreme" (or book of the Duchess), gives a very full account of his patron's devotion to Blanche, and his grief at her death. He depicts John of Gaunt as —

"A wondir faire welfaring Knight,
By the manir me thoughten so
Of gode mokil, right yonge thereto,
Of the age of foure and twenty yere
Upon his berde but litil here. [1]
 \* \* \* \* \*
And with a dedly so'rowful sowne
He made of rime ten verses or twelve
Of a complainte unto himselve,
The most pite, and the most routhe,
That evir I herde, for by trouthe
It was grete wondir that nature
Might suffire any creature
To have soche sorow', and he not ded." [2]

By degrees the knight tells the tale of his loss with bitter lamentations, "for I am sorowe' and sorowe' is I," [3] dwelling with yearning tenderness on the beauty and virtues of his lost wife: —

"For certis she was that swete wife
My suffisaunce, my luste, my life,
Min hope, min hele, and al my blesse.
My world's welfare, and my goddesse,
And I wholly hers and every dele." [4]

And when the poet declares his full belief that in the eyes of the knight she seemed to be the fairest of all women, he is almost indignantly interrupted:-

"With myn! nay all whiche that her seyen,
Sayid and swore that it was so." [5]

It is useless to multiply quotations to show from such a trustworthy source that John of Gaunt cherished his first wife with true love, and sincerely mourned her death. That his third marriage was also one of affection is tolerably clear from the fact that the. lady had been his mistress for many years, and was not of high birth, so that he would hardly have married her, had he not really loved her. His second marriage is usually regarded as one of mere ambition, in want of any proof to the contrary.

His children were eight in number, [Y3] and three of them became sovereigns; Henry of England, Philippa of Portugal, and Catherine of Castile and Leon. We know very little of his domestic relations, but if Shakespeare has taken a right view in his play of Richard II., he cannot have had much affection for his eldest son, or he would hardly have given him the cold-blooded advice to remain content with his fate.

He was passionately fond of hunting, and several notices of his following this pursuit at Hatfield [Z3] in Yorkshire, at Leicester, and. at Tutbury, are still extant. Indeed, at the last-named place, he appointed a court to be held every year on the day (Aug. 16th) after the festival of the Assumption, to elect a King of the Minstrels, and to promote festivities, with various ceremonies. The wood master and rangers of Needwood Forest, after holding their annual meeting, rode in procession through the town, and finished up the day with merry sports, some of them, unfortunately, too much in accordance with the barbarous taste of the times, A full and most interesting account of these proceedings is given in the second volume of Chambers' "Book of Days," p. 224.

The story of John of Gaunt's liberality to some persons who held allotments in the parish of Ratby, in Leicestershire, testifies to his feeling interest in the humble concerns of the people, though it is to be regretted that he showed it in this case in a spirit of rather coarse humour. [6] The same tendency marked the order of proceeding at Tutbury, but too much stress should not be laid upon it, as the habits of that age were so different to those of the present.

On the whole, then, the general opinion passed by men on John of Gaunt would seem to be correct. He cannot be absolved of forming plans for securing the throne of England for himself, though I think he was not guilty of meditating treason against the reigning King. Unable to cope with statesmen like William of Wykeham in ability and tact, he yet managed to hold his own, by virtue of his position as a wealthy Prince of the royal blood. Without the power of restraining the violence of his anger, he was led into acts which completely alienated the people, and few Princes have been so unpopular.

He was a thoroughly disappointed man, and could hardly have experienced much happiness in the reflection that he was distasteful both to the Court and to the people. All this, combined with illness contracted in Spain, may well have brought his life to a close earlier than the usual course of nature. We are too apt to take our idea of his age when he died, from Shakespeare, who speaks of "time-honoured Lancaster," as an old and venerable man, foretelling the ruin of his country with prophetic vision: but yet he was only 59 years of age at his death. Happy in that he did not live to see his fondest hopes shattered by the elevation of another to the throne which he had so much coveted, but from which .his unpopularity would ever have debarred him, he leaves behind him the reputation of being a typical Englishman of his times, whose many faults and failings, exaggerated as they doubtless were by his sworn enemies, the monkish historians of the period, are largely condoned by his gallant bearing against the foes of his country, who early learnt to respect and fear the warlike son of a warlike sire.

[1] Line 452, Urry's Chaucer.
[2] Line 462.
[3] Line 507.
[4] Line 1037.
[5] Line 1052.
[6] Godwin's Life of Chaucer III., 337.

Throsby's Leicestershire. Art. Ratby.

# Chief Authorities

Baines.   History of Lancashire.   Edit. 1868.
Barnes.   Life of Edward III.   Edit. 1688.
Beltz.   Memorials of the Order of the Garter.   Edit. 1841.
Bouchet.   Annals of Aquitaine.   Edit. 1644.
Camden.   Britannia.   Edit. 1637.
Capgrave.   Chronicles of England.   Edit. 1863. (Rolls' Collection.)
Collins.   Life of John of Gaunt.   Edit. 1740.
Daniel.   History of England.   Edit. 1634.
Froissart.   Chronicles. Edit.   1812.
Godwin.   Life of Chaucer.   Edit. 1804.
Gregson.   History of Lancashire.   Edit. 1817.
Hardy.   Charters granted to Dukes of Lancaster.   Edit. 1845.
Holinshed.   Chronicles.   Edit. 1807.
Hook.   Lives of the Archbishops of Canterbury.   Edit. 1860.
Knighton.   Historise Anglicanae Scriptores Decem. (Twysden, vol. II.) Edit. 1652.
Lewis.   Life of Wickliffe.   Edit. 1820.
Lingard.   History of England.   Edit. 1854.
Lowth.   Life of William of Wykeham.   Edit. 1759.
Milman.   Annals of St. Paul's.   Edit. 1868.
Milman.   History of Latin Christianity.   Edit. 1855.
Nicolas.   History of the Royal Navy.   Edit. 1847.
Rymer.   Foedera.   Edit. 1704.
Sandford.   Genealogical History of England.   Edit. 1677.
Stow.   Annals.   Edit. 1601.
Walsingham.   Historia Anglicana.   Edit. 1863. (Rolls' Collection.)
Wright.   Political Songs.   Edit. 1859. (Rolls' Collection.)

# Appendix

**[A]** In 1319, the French Bishops were expelled by an ordinance from the Parliament of Paris. It should be remembered here that the functions of these French Parliaments were judicial, not legislative.

**[B]** Grosseteste, the eminent Bishop of Lincoln, gives this picture of the morals of the clergy. "Nos...tam multiplicia mala, tam gravia, tam deformia, tam faeda, tam flagitiosa, tam facinorosa, tam sacrilega, populo Christi cruore redempto universaliter inesse, et inhoerere, neglectu rectorum, et incuria pastorum, et quod heu! fiendum est potius quam scribendum; et exemplo pessimo, et pernicie rabida et impudenter ubique serpente; cernimus evidenter." Luard's Ed. Grosseteste's Epistola, preface, p. 24. Also cf. Wright's Political Songs, i., 257 (on the council of London, A.D. 1382), 264.

**[C]** Prologue to the Canterbury Tales, p. 28. (Tyrwhit's Chaucer, 2nd Ed.) Cf.
"Syr Davyde Lyndesay of the Mount, Lord Lyon, Kinge at Armes."
"I am Schir Robert Rome — raker
Ane perfyte publick pardoner
    Admittit by the Pape;
Sirs, I shall shaw you, for my wage
My pardons and my pilgrimage
    Quhilk ye sail see and grape,
I give to the devill with gude intent.
This unsell (evil) wickit New Testament,
    With thame that it translaitit,
Sen layik men knew the veritee
Pardoners getis no charitee
    Without that they debait it."
— Chalmers' Lyndesay, n., 10.

**[D]** Cf. St. Palaye Mém. Sur la Chevalerie. Hallam's History of the Middle Ages, III., 482. Sismondi de Sismondi "Midi de l'Europe" says, "The more we study history the more we shall be convinced that chivalry is a poetical invention. We never can arrive by any authentic documents at the scene where it flourished. It is always represented at a distance both of time and place. While contemporary historians give us a distinct idea of the vices of courts, and of the great, of the ferocity of nobles, and the degradation of the people, we see, after a lapse of time, the same ages animated by the poets with splendid accounts of virtue, beauty, and loyalty."

[E] Henry Taylor's play of Philip van Artevelde is very instructive on these points.

[F] "Watte vocat, cui Thome venit, neque Symme retardat,
    Betteque Gibbe simul Hykke venire jubet,
  Colle furit, que Gibbe juvat nocumenta parantes.
    Cum quibus ad damnum Wille coire vovet,
  Grigge rapit, dum Davve strepit, comes est quibus Hobbe,
    Lorkin et in medio non minor esse putat,
  Hudde ferit, quos Judde terit, dum Tebbe juvatur,
    Jakke domosque viros vellit, et ense necat." — John Gower.

[G] Warden on Consular Establishments. Macpherson (Annals of Commerce i., 536) says the first notice of an English Consul is in 1346.

[H] The exact date is uncertain. Stow and Barnes (i. 14, § 2-3) whose date is accepted by Godwin, say, "about the beginning of Februarie." Holinshed, ii., 612, says, "he was borne about Christmasse in the 13th yere of King Edward's reigne." Neither Walsingham nor Capgrave specify the day in any way, but Baines, in his History of Lancashire, boldly declares, without giving any reference to his authorities, that John was born between March 25th and 31st. All we know for certain is, that his birth took place during Edward's absence in England, where he arrived February 21st, and shortly after his departure from Ghent.

[I] Froissart says, Edward was in such a hurry to get to Scotland, that he went from Dover direct without passing through London; this is erroneous, as Edward was present in Parliament November 25th. Nicolas Hist. Royal Navy, ii. 120.

[J] David Bruce was the true King of Scotland; he had been a prisoner in England since the battle of Neville's Cross (1346), and was ransomed for 100,000 marks (Capgrave, 218) in 1357. Walsingham says (i. 284) he had also to pay the expenses of his imprisonment.

[K] The household accounts of the first wife of Lionel from 1356-9 were found on the cover of additional MS 18632 in the British Museum. See E. A. Bond, in the "Fortnightly Review" for August, 1866.

[L] Lancaster had gone to France June 18th, 1357.

[M] Grant to John in special tail of the castle and lordship of Lydell in Northumberland.

[N] Cf. Beltz Memorials of the Order of the Garter 132, 599. John was 37th Knight (26 founders). He was succeeded by Sir Philip de la Vache (93rd Knight). Cf. also Ashmole, 708.

[O] Grant to John, Earl of Lancaster and Richmond, and Blanche, his wife, and the heirs of their two bodies, of certain liberties in the lands and fees of the said Blanche, one of the co-heirs of Henry, late Duke of Lancaster, after the petition made between her and her sister Matilda (Maud?) — viz., return of writs, pleas of withernam, fines and amercements, chattels of felons and fugitives. Charters of Duchy of Lancaster, ed. by W. Hardy.

[P] For a list of his land and manors, see Collins' Life of John of Gaunt, p. 6. Baines' Hist, of Lancashire, pages 109, 110.

[Q] Barnes (III., VII., § 8) adopts Knighton's view.

[R] The title of Duke had only been conferred twice before— viz., on the Black Prince and Henry of Lancaster.

[S] July 14th, 1364. Recital of Charter of May 7th, 1342, to Henry, Earl of Lancaster, and of surrender thereof by the son and heir of the grantee; and further recital that the grant so made in fee tail could not legally be annulled. The said charter of liberties renewed in favour of John, Duke of Lancaster, and Blanche, his wife, daughter and heir of Henry, the late Duke — viz., acquittance of tolls, &c., return of writs, and summons of the exchequer; amercements, forfeited issues, forfeitures, &c. Memorandum on the Charter Roll of July 14th, 1364, shewing the limitation of the above grant to the lands which belonged to the Earl of Lancaster on May 7th, 1342.

[T] A religious colour was given the expedition by asserting it was a crusade against the Moors at Grenada.

[U] The ballad on Prince Edward's expedition to Spain, by Walter of Peterborough (p. 103 Wright's Ballads). John of Gaunt had been with the Black Prince before, and had been sent by him to England to obtain the King's advices, but the allusion is too indefinite to be depended upon without further authority, which at present is not forthcoming.

[V] Pedro offered 550,000 florins to the Companies, and 56,000 to Edward, with the lordship of Biscay in addition.

[W] Walsingham describes Pedro as "pessimus maleficus et tyrannus, proscribens et interficiens suos naturales homines. Et quod pejus, spretâ religione Christianâ, cum quâdam se Judaeâ foeminâ miscuisset." The relative importance of his faults is truly monkish; no wonder the Pope excommunicated him. — Froissart, vol. i., c. 229.

[X] Many Frenchmen fought against Pedro "partim missi per Regem Francioe, partim lucri contemplatione." — Walsingham, I., 304.

[Y] Walsingham (i., 304) says John of Gaunt and Chandos commanded those "qui de Magnâ Comitivâ adhoeserunt Principi."

[Z] "The vanguard of the army was ordered with wonderful discretion, and there stood John of Gaunt, Duke of Lancaster, in the flower of his youth, being at that time in the 27th year of his age, of great strength, conduct and courage, and honourably emulous of his brother Prince Edward's glory." — Barnes, 501.

[A2] According to Froissart, John said to one of the Earl of Warwick's sons at the battle of Najara, "Sir William, there is the enemy; you shall see me to-day prove myself a true knight, or you shall see me lost in the attempt."

[B2] The Castillian nobles before the Battle of Najara counselled Enrique to fight for fear of a revolt, which shows the people were not so opposed to Pedro as is usually represented; they were probably indifferent to either Prince, with a leaning to right succession. — Cf. Sismondi's Hist, de France, xi., 38-46.

[C2] Collins says this force consisted of 300 men-at-arms, 500 archers, 3 bannerets, 80 knights, 216 squires; the Castle of Becherell was pawned to King Edward for money to carry on the wars.

[D2] John of Gaunt's third wife was the poet's sister-in-law.

[E2] Lionel had died in Italy, 1368.

[F2] These Princesses were illegitimate daughters of Pedro by the celebrated Marie Padilla; he afterwards swore he had married her, and declared her daughters his heirs.

[G2] In the register of John of Gaunt, the Edward III., remaining in that office, there is the entry of an instrument dated Bordeaux, July 21st, 1371, declaring the relinquishment by John of the lieutenancy of Aquitaine with the consent of the Chamber of Parliament at Bordeaux, into the charge of John de Greylly, Captal de Buche, the constable, and Thomas de Felton, the seneschal, the conations of his appointment thereto by the Black Prince not having been fulfilled. What these conditions were I have not been able to discover.

[H2] Hook (Lives of the Archbishops of Canterbury, iv., 232) says, Alice Perrers wrote to the sheriff in the King's name, and they influenced the electors so much, that a Lancastrian Parliament was returned.

[I2] Wickliffe bitterly alludes to Wykeham in the following words: "Benefices instead of being bestowed on poor clerks, are heaped on a kitchen clerk, or one wise in building castles or in worldly business." Wykeham was the architect of Windsor Castle. — Cf. Vaughan i., 312; Milman's Hist. Lat. Christ, vi., 109.

[J2] His resumé of the proceedings in Parliament on this occasion is the first known instance of Parliamentary reporting.

[K2] Edward was wont to complain that he never knew a King fight so little and yet give so much trouble.

[L2] "And after he was go, alle the countre turned Frensch save Burdews and Bayon."— Capgrave, 229.

[M2] Walsingham i., 318, says the French duped the English and played at negotiations while new weapons were being made.

[N2] The Papal legates were the Bishops of Pampeluna and Sinigaglia.

[O2] The accounts in the Exchequer show Wickliffe was absent from July 27 to Sept. 14. He received £60 for his expenses at 20s. per day; for passage 50s., for re-passage 42s. 3d., quoted in Preface to Wickliffe's Bible, Oxford, p. vii. — Milman's Hist. Lat. Christ, vi., 112.

[P2] Walsingham, Capgrave, and other historians accuse her of continually interfering in the Law Courts.

[Q2] 1376. The King gave John in special tail the town and Castle of Bergeriac, in the diocese of Perigort, in France, to hold in as ample a manner as Henry, Duke of Lancaster enjoyed.

[R2] "And that he might get the people's favour, he moved the King to give the said goods to the Prince called Richard of Bordeaux, and he used the young Prince's name for his owne helpe." — Stow, p. 429.

[S2] Richard, Prince of Wales, opened it. He had also been created Earl of Chester and Duke of Cornwall.

[T2] "In this tyme on Jon Wiclef, Maystir of Oxenforth, held many straunge opiniones: That the Cherch of Rome is not hed of alle Cherchis: That Peter had no more auctorite thanne the other Aposteles: ne the Pope no more power than anothir prest. And that temporal lordes may take away the godes from the Cherch, whan the persones trespasin. And that no reules mad be Augustin, Benet and Fraunceys, adde no more perfeccion over the Gospel, than doth lym whiting onto a wal. And that bischoppis schuld have no prisones, and many other thingis." — Capgrave, 231. Cf. also Walsingham i., 324, 353.

[U2] Godwin says the story of John of Gaunt proposing to introduce military laws into the city, was a fabrication of his enemies, but it seems to be the truth.

[V2] Feb. 28. — Grant to John, King of Castile and Leon, Duke of Lancaster, for life, of a Court of Chancery, Chancellor, justices, cognisance of pleas, and other jura regalia in the County of Lancaster which pertain to a County Palatine, as freely as the Earl of Chester enjoyed the same in the County of Chester. Reservation to the Crown of all tenths, fifteenths, and other subsidies and taxes granted by Parliament, and of the power of pardoning life, with Superiority and correction of errors or defect of justice in the Courts of the Duke of Lancaster. The said Duke to send knights of the shire and burgesses to serve in Parliament, and to appoint collectors of parliamentary taxes and subsidies.

"Ut habeat infra Comitatem Lancastriae cancellariam suam, ac Brevia sua sub sigillo suo pro officio, Cancellarii, deportando, consignando, Justiciarios suos tam ad placita Coronae quam ad quaecunque alia placita Communem Legem tangentia, tenenda, ac cognitiones eorundem et quascunque Executiones per Brevia sua et ministros suos faciendas." — Rot. Pat. A. 50 Edw. III. (Quoted in Nicolson's Eng. Hist. Library, III., 110.)

[W2] June 4. — Grant giving same liberties to John of Gaunt in some of the lands he received in exchange for the Earldom of Richmond, but which were not mentioned by name (only in valuation), as he had in those named — *i.e.*, knights, fees, advowsons, wardships, marriages, escheats, chases, parks, &c.

[X2] A portrait of John of Gaunt in this capacity is preserved in the Cottonian MSS. in the British Museum. He is dressed in dark blue and white; a figure, supposed to represent Thomas of Woodstock, High Constable of England, is kneeling at his feet, in dark blue and red; the seat is a kind of pink, the background red, while a letter in his hand is half blue and half red, worked on with white, and blue covers with a gold edge round the whole. — Strutt's Regal and Ecclesiastical Ant., p. 42, plate 16.

**[Y2]** Brest was ceded to the English by John de Montfort, Duke of Brittany, in return for their help. The King of Navarre, who was now at war with France, had ceded to them the town and port of Cherbourg in return for assistance. De Montfort married Edward III.'s fourth daughter, Mary.

**[Z2]** Nov. 10th, 1378.— Recital of Grant of County Palatine to John, King of Castile and Leon, Duke of Lancaster, and that the grantee had subsequently petitioned the King to have the general words specially expressed on certain points; the said general words therefore declared to embrace the 'powers exercised by the Duke in virtue thereof— viz., to have his Exchequer and Barons thereof in the County Palatine, and the appointment of justices of the forest except in pleas arising where the Crown is a party.

**[A3]** In 1384 Katherine of Lancaster, daughter of Constance of Castile, is also included; and in 1386, 1389, 1396, 1399, we find mention of the daughters of John of Gaunt attending the feast, Joan de Beaufort appearing for the first time in 1399. Lady Katherine de Swinford was invited in 1387; in her case the robes seem to have been issued at first without authority, as the sanction of letters under the Privy Seal, dated Aug. 8 following, appear to have been necessary. She is, however, therein fully recognised as "de secta *aliarum* dominarum de eadem societate (de Garterio)." — Beltz, Memorials of the Order of the Garter, ad. ann., and p. 250, n. 6.

**[B3]** This tax is often confused with the poll tax of 1379, which was graduated from John of Gaunt and the Archbishop of Canterbury at £6 13s. 4d., to the labourer or poor man at 4d. This failed to suffice for the requirements of the State, to meet which another poll tax was levied, the collection of which caused the rebellion of 1381. The words of the declaration from the Rolls, p. 90, are — "De chacun laie personne, si bien des madles, come des females, qui sont passey l'age de XV. ans trois groats."

**[C3]** The Savoy Palace was built by Peter, Earl of Savoy and Richmond, on whose death it escheated to the Crown; and Henry III. conferred it on his son, Edmund Crouchback, through whom it became a possession of the Earls of Lancaster.

**[D3]** Besides the Savoy the insurgents burnt the temple and hospital of the Knights of St. John of Jerusalem. Wat Tyler is supposed to have been in command at the burning of the Savoy, some say Jack Straw. Froissart (i. 273) says they were both present. These two were often confounded, indeed Holinshed and Knighton say they were the same person "whose right name was Wat Tyler, which he had now changed into Jack Strawe." Stow says that Wat Tyler was killed at Smithfield, while Jack Straw, whose dying confession he gives, was executed. A political squib of the period says Jack Straw was killed at Smithfield.

"Our Kyng hadde no rest,
   Alii latuere caverna
To ride he was ful prest,
   Recolendo gesta paterna
Jack Straw down he kest
   Smythfield virtute superna.
Lord, as thou may best,
   Regem defende, guberna."

Wright's Pol. Songs, i., 226, Rolls' Collection.

Fabian follows this ballad. There was a painting of Sir W. Walworth, according to the "Citizens' Chronicle" (pub. 1827), in the possession of that Earl of Leicester who died in 1743, having the following inscription on it: — "This. is. the. pictor. of. Sir. William. Walworth. Knight. That, kylde. Jake. Strawe. the. rebel, in. Kynge. Richard's, sight."

The confusion appears hopeless, and it must be left to the reader to decide whether there were two distinct men, or whether they were one and the same; if the latter supposition is adopted, we must suppose that some one assumed the name Jack Straw again, that is if we credit Stow's account of a Jack Straw. Shakespeare, by the way, has a strange anachronism in his play Henry VI. (2nd part), act iv. scene 7; for he there makes Jack Cade bid his followers destroy the Savoy.

[E3] John Cote's confession about John of Gaunt, Oct. 7th. - Archaeologia Cantiana, iv.

[F3] Froissart, x., c. 375-6. Rymer vii., 323. 6 Richard II., Aug. 8, 1381. Walsingham, Buchanan, Knighton, and Collins, say he spent some *months* in Edinburgh; if they are correct he could not have returned to England till nearly November, as he certainly did not go to Edinburgh till the end of June. Godwin, in his "Life of Chaucer" takes a different view from the above authorities, and in my text I have inclined to this view.

**[G3]** Collins says wrongly that John of Gaunt did go, and in order to make it possible, coolly assigns 1382 as the proper date of the expedition.

**[H3]** Wickliffe soon after retired to Lutterworth, where he died Dec. 31st, 1384, and is consigned by Walsingham to the companionship of Cain! Capgrave, p. 240, abuses him roundly as the "orgon of the devil, the enmy of the Church, the confusion of men, the ydol of heresie, the meroure of ypocrisie, the norischer of scisme."

**[I3]** The rest of this proclamation reveals a sad picture of the dissoluteness prevailing in the County of Lancaster; it observes that so licentious had become the public manners, that the female character was treated with the greatest disrespect, and "ladies and the noble maids and women" were frequently violated by force, and these ladies resented it so little as to marry their ravishers; therefore, if, after such outrage, the parties contracted marriage, the parties shall both of them be disabled — ipso facto — from maintaining any inheritance, dowry, or conjoint feoffment, or from receiving any bequest from their ancestors, and that the inheritance should descend to the next in blood.— Cf. Scot. 7 Rich. II., m, 1. (Baines' Hist. Lancashire.)

**[J3]** "And in the same yere, before Lenton, the same Duke, with Thomas, erl of Bokyngam, his brother, and with a great noumbyr, went into Scotlond. That aspied of Scottis, thei fled ovir the se, and summe hid hem in forestis. So the Englisch host was fayn to com hom ageyn, compelled for cold and hungir." — Capgrave, p. 240. "And did little good," Stow ad. ann. Also cf. Walsingham II., 111.

**[K3]** He left his son, Henry of Derby, with a council, in charge of his English possessions. Froissart is wrong in saying he left Bristol in May. — Cf, Nicolas, Hist. British Navy. He was some time at Plymouth before he started, for "at the palace of John of Gaunt, King of Castile and Leon, in the convent of the Friars Carmelites, at Plymouth," we find him giving his testimony in favour of the right of Sir Richard Scrope to the arms borne by him, in the celebrated controversy between Sir Richard Scrope and Sir Richard Grosvenor. — Scrope and Grosvenor Roll, p. 49.

**[L3]** Knighton, Collins, Sandford, and Stow, say his force consisted of 20,000 men, of whom 2,000 were men-at-arms, and 8,000 were archers. Baines, in his History of Lancashire, says he went with 1,000 knights and esquires, 2,000 archers, and 1,000 tall yeomen. The Pope supported his enterprise, "and because that Spaynardis were scismatikes, the Pope Urban graunted every man in that viage plener remission of synne that wold go with the Duke or gyve ony good to his viage." — Capgrave, p. 242.

[M3] Twelve lords, 80 knights, 200 squires, and over 500 soldiers, are said to have perished. Cf. Lodge's Peerage under Lord Windsor, Sir James Windsor having been with John of Gaunt.

[N3] Froissart, Walsingham, Collins, and Biondi are wrong in saying this was withdrawn from him; he is described as Duke of Aquitaine in a patent after his death. Camden, in his Britannia, p. 757, says Henry IV. bestowed this title on his eldest son.

[O3] This is Godwin's account as well as Sandford's. Collins says he was to receive £200,000, and £10,000 during his and his wife's life. Edmund of York, and his heirs, were to succeed to the throne of Castile, if no heirs were born to Henry and Catherine. Knighton more reasonably says he stipulated for 16,000 marks for himself, and 12,000 marks for his wife; the same authority asserts he only brought away half the indemnity, and perhaps the pensions were never paid. The Encyclopedia Metropolitana fixes the sum at 60,000 francs, with 4,000 annually to Constance, and four towns in fief. The Harl. MSS., cod. 266, fo. 986 (quoted in Baines' Hist. Lanc., p. 119), says the King of Spain gave him "of gold and silver that were cast into two great ingots, as much as eight chariots might carry, and many other rich jewels and gifts," also 10,000 marks, to be paid yearly into Bayonne to the Duke's assign, the expense and risk of transit to be borne by Spain.

[P3] This lady, the widow of Sir Hugh Swinford, was the daughter of Paganus de Rouet, or Roet, a native of Hainault, and king-at-arms for the province of Guienne. Her husband died in 1372, and we first hear of her as John of Gaunt's mistress in 1377; she had been his first wife's attendant, and latterly governess to his children. She died May 10th, 1403, and was buried at Lincoln, where her daughter Joan also lies.

[Q3] June 29th, 1396. Confirmation by inspeximus of the charters of May 12th, 1362, and Sept. 15th, 1377 (two on the same day), notwithstanding non-user and without let from any of the King's bailiffs or ministers. The merits of the grantee, John, Duke of Lancaster, the King's uncle, being a consideration for more ample grace, the King grants to him for the term of his life, certain additional liberties, — viz., all fines for trespass, praefines, and posfines, ransoms, amercements, forfeited issues, forfeitures, year, day, and waste, imposed or adjudged in any Court, as fully as the King would have them, if not granted to the said Duke, and the Duke may levy the same by his own officers, by estreats to be delivered to them, without let from the King's officers; assay and assize of bread and other matters belonging to the office of clerk of the market; chattels of felons and fugitives, and may seize the same without let from the King's bailiffs or ministers; return and execution of writs, summons, estreats, and precepts, attachment of pleas of the Crown; no sheriff or other bailiff of the King may intromit, unless in default. Fines and amercements of sheriffs and bailiffs of liberties for negligence; waifs and strays, deodands, treasure troves, mainour; saving of liberties before granted in fee tail.

[R3] Capgrave, p. 266, cf., the Deposition of Halle. Gower, in his "Vox Clamantis," says:

"Heu quam tortorum quidam de sorte malorum,
Sic Ducis electi plumarum pondere lecti,
Corpus quassatum jugulantque necant jugulatum."

[S3] Froissart vol. ii., c. 228-9, gives as the true version of the affair the exact opposite of this. It should be remembered that Bolingbroke and Thomas had married sisters, co-heiresses of the family of Bohun, Earls of Hereford.

[T3] Cf. Dr. Gascoigne, Dictionarium Theologicum apud MSS. in Line. Coll., Oxon. Also Anthony d Wood, A.D. 1484, both quoted by Godwin.

[U3] Froissart, II., 163 (99). "He was hymselfe soo wery and hevy that gladly he wolde have layen in his bedde, and it had nat ben for discoragynge of his people."

[V3] King Richard II., act i., scene 2:—

"For I may never lift
An angry arm against His minister."

[W3] In Fasciculi Zizaniorum, p. 292, we find, "Epistola vel litera quatuor ordinum Claustralium Oxoniae ad dominum Johannem ducem Lancastriae contra Magistrum Nicolaum Herforde et alios pacem perturbantes. (By stirring up all ranks against the mendicant orders.) They clearly did not consider John of Gaunt a true follower of Wickliffe.

**[X3]** His bravery grew into a proverb of Shakespeare. — 1 Henry IV., II., 2.

*P. Henry.* — What, a coward, Sir John Paunch?

*Falstaff.* — Indeed, I am not John of Gaunt, your grandfather; but yet no coward, Hal.

**[Y3]** I. By Blanche of Lancaster.

(1.) Henry of Lancaster, surnamed Bolingbroke (Henry IV.)

(2.) Philippa, Queen of Portugal.

(3.) Elizabeth, Duchess of Exeter.

II. By Constance of Castile and Leon.

(4.) Catherine, Queen of Castile and Leon.

III. By Catherine Swinford.

(5.) John Beaufort, Earl of Somerset.

(6.) Henry Beaufort, Cardinal of St. Eusebius and Bishop of Winchester.

(7.) Thomas Beaufort, Duke of Exeter and Earl of Dorset.

(8.) Joan Beaufort, Countess of Westmoreland.

**[Z3]** He rode over to Hatfield from his official residence at Lincoln, which is famous for its beautiful oriel window.

www.ingramcontent.com/pod-product-compliance
Lightning Source LLC
Chambersburg PA
CBHW031427040426
42444CB00006B/711